Meeting Wise

Meeting Wise

Making the Most of Collaborative Time for Educators

Kathryn Parker Boudett
Elizabeth A. City

Harvard Education Press
Cambridge, Massachusetts

Fourth Printing, 2016

Library of Congress Control Number 2014932482

Paperback ISBN 978-1-61250-694-4
Library Edition 978-1-61250-695-1

Published by Harvard Education Press,
an imprint of the Harvard Education Publishing Group

Harvard Education Press
8 Story Street
Cambridge, MA 02138

Cover Design: Ciano Design
Cover Photos Getty Images: Hong Li/E+ (paper texture);
hudiemm/E+ (checklist)
The typefaces used in this book are Minion Pro, Myriad Pro,
Gill Sans, and Museo Slab.

For Dick Murnane
beloved mentor
and master collaborator

CONTENTS

ACKNOWLEDGMENTS

We are thankful:

to Candice Bocala, Eva Mejia, Richard Murnane, David Rease Jr., and Michele Shannon for showing us what good meetings look and sound and feel like;

to Heather Ayres, Karla Baehr, Cynthia Boudett, Rose DiTullio, Matthew Miller, Ann Marie Parker, Stefanie Reinhorn, and especially our editor at Harvard Education Press, Caroline Chauncey, for helping us put that experience into words;

to the educators from around the world who have embraced the Meeting Wise Checklist, tried it themselves, and shared their insights so we could adapt and adjust;

to Mike, Dorothy, Eliza, Shannon, Chris, and Maggie for their loving support of this collaboration and for reminding us how joyful learning together can be;

and most of all: to children everywhere, for inspiring us every day to use every minute of collaborative time wisely.

INTRODUCTION

THIS LITTLE BOOK CONTAINS one big idea that has transformed our practice and that of many educators we work with: *meetings matter.* Every day, millions of people gather in classrooms, faculty rooms, boardrooms, and (sometimes virtual) conference rooms to tackle problems that are so big that no individual can solve them alone. How to prepare students to thrive in a knowledge economy and rapidly developing world, how to support teachers in transforming their practice, how to create policy that drives opportunity and access for every learner—addressing each of these would truly make a big difference in learning and teaching. But although some of the meetings that *could* take on these issues are invigorating opportunities for generating ideas and creating solutions, many are not.

Have you ever had to sit through a whole hour when you felt that the substance of the meeting could have been handled in five minutes? Or planned a thoughtful meeting only to have it derailed by a couple of rogue participants who had their own agendas? Have you ever felt that the meetings you are expected to lead (or the ones you are obligated to attend) get in the way of the "real work" that you need to do? If so, we hope this book gives you a new way of thinking about and working with your collaborative time.

But first, let us introduce ourselves. We are Kathy Boudett and Liz City, faculty members at the Harvard Graduate School of Education (HGSE) who have a longtime fascination with understanding what makes people work together effectively. One fun fact is that we first encountered each another at a meeting. The conversation was facilitated by our beloved mentor, Richard Murnane, who was teaching a course for Boston Public Schools principals and teachers and HGSE graduate students. The seeds were planted that day for the creation of *Data Wise: A Step-by-Step Guide to Using Assessment Results to Improve Teaching and Learning*, which the three of us wrote with sixteen other researchers and practitioners over the following two years.[1] We learned much as we figured out how to make the regular meetings of our diverse group productive and a source of joy and growth for all involved.

Since we first published that book in 2005, Kathy has gone on to establish and direct the Data Wise Project at HGSE, which is dedicated to supporting schools and districts in using a wide range of data sources to improve learning and teaching. Helping educators transform their approach to meetings has become a central component of her work; she has been energized by the determination many educators have shown in ushering in a "whole new way of doing business" in their organizations.

In the meantime, Liz has worked with colleagues to develop the practice of instructional rounds to improve learning and teaching.[2] She has also worked with superintendents and other leaders to become more strategic and focused in their improvement work. Most recently, Liz codesigned the Doctor of Education Leadership (Ed.L.D.) Program at HGSE and now serves as its director. In her current role and as a former teacher and principal, Liz has seen what meetings look like throughout the educational sector. She sees time and again how no one person can accomplish the task of helping every child learn and how deliberate attention to the quality of collaboration at every level of the system can make a huge difference in the lived experience of both adults and children.

Our combined experience has led both of us to believe that meetings—precisely because there is so much room for improvement in their quality—provide a great opportunity for supporting educators not just in learning to work together but in *learning to learn*. We have thus developed very specific strategies for making meetings better. The goal of this book is to distill our insights into a concise format that can be digested on a plane ride, a lazy Sunday afternoon, or over a week of determined stints on an exercise bike.

We have written other books that deal with the challenge of transforming educational cultures and describe processes that can take years to fully establish. This book differs from those because it offers ideas that you can put into practice right away. In fact, if you happen to be hosting or participating in a meeting this week, you could start making changes as early as tomorrow.

OVERVIEW OF THE BOOK

First, a note: when we talk about meetings throughout this book, we are mostly referring to recurring meetings that take place with a relatively consistent group of people over a period of time. Examples include school board meetings, faculty meetings, team meetings, planning meetings, ongoing professional development sessions, and parent/teacher conferences for monitoring individualized education programs. While we hope you find our recommendations relevant to your experience with ad hoc meetings, we're especially interested in enabling groups that convene regularly to make significant progress on their goals by making more effective use of ongoing collaborative time.

Section I of the book is an invitation to think differently about meetings. Chapter 1 encourages you to appreciate the untapped potential that lies within each appointment blocked on your calendar and describes the importance of making thoughtful investments of time in adult—and, ultimately, student—learning.

The transformation begins with thoughtful planning. Chapter 2 describes a simple but powerful tool for improving the quality of agendas: the Meeting Wise Checklist. Meant as a reflective guide, this tool comprises twelve questions that push you and your colleagues to get crystal clear about *what* a particular meeting is designed to achieve and *how* to best achieve it.

Chapter 3 shows how the Meeting Wise Checklist can be applied in a range of meetings, and the changes that result. Drawing on examples from meetings that vary widely in terms of size, frequency, power dynamic, and level within the educational system, the chapter takes a peek behind the curtain. It shows the kinds of conversations that the checklist is designed to generate and points you toward specific things you can do to make your own meetings more effective. The chapter concludes with a sample agenda template that embodies the checklist.

Section II shifts from *thinking* differently about meetings to *working* differently. Our ultimate goal is to improve student learning through improved collaboration, which means moving from deliberate thought to action.

Chapter 4 describes the essential foundational tasks that set meetings and groups up for success, including everything from establishing group norms and developing systems for tracking the work over time to nitty-gritty recurring tasks, like taking care of logistics.

Because there is a lot more to an effective meeting than the planning that goes into it, the next two chapters focus on what happens as the meeting unfolds, highlighting specific things that facilitators (chapter 5) and participants (chapter 6) can do in the heat of the moment. These chapters offer strategies for keeping to (and deviating from) the agenda, supporting full engagement, managing conflict, and maintaining awareness of the role you play within the group. Each chapter offers "top tips" for things facilitators and participants can regularly do to contribute to a productive meeting, as well as a list of "common dilemmas" and what to do about them. By addressing the meeting experience from both the facilitator and participant point of view, these chapters provide language and ideas that prepare you and your colleagues to anticipate and frame challenges before a meeting. They also are designed to support you in reflecting afterward and engaging in a candid discussion of what worked, what didn't, and what you individually and collectively can do about it.

Chapter 7 shows how groups and organizations can become meeting wise over time, explaining how different components of the book can be used to help you to find an entry point and get started from wherever your meetings are now.

Woven throughout the book are "Try It Yourself" exercises for practical application of the tools and key ideas. While most of these are exercises to be done on your own or with a colleague, in chapter 7, there are "Try It *Yourselves*" exercises to do with a group of colleagues to make collective commitments for improving meetings. (See "Index of 'Try It Yourself' Activities" that follows.)

The book concludes with a number of resources, including a list of selected readings, citations to or step-by-step instructions for many of the protocols mentioned, and full versions of the key tools.

Index of "Try It Yourself" Activities		
CHAPTER 1	Estimate the Cost of Meetings	p. 11
	Rate the Quality of Your Meetings	p. 12
	Describe Terrible and Great Meetings	p. 14
CHAPTER 2	Use the Checklist to Review Agendas	p. 37
CHAPTER 3	Use the Checklist to Design an Agenda	p. 70
CHAPTER 4	Set Yourself Up for Success	p. 83
CHAPTER 5	Test-Drive Facilitation Tips	p. 118
CHAPTER 6	Test-Drive Participation Tips	p. 139
CHAPTER 7	Make a Collective Commitment to . . .	
	• Creating Better Agendas	p. 144
	• Investing in a Firmer Foundation	p. 145
	• Facilitating and Participating More Effectively	p. 147
	• Addressing a Meeting Dilemma	p. 148

HOW TO USE THIS BOOK

Whether you are a teacher, a state commissioner of education, a principal, a superintendent, a parent, a school board member, a leader of a community organization, an education entrepreneur, or another contributor in education, we hope you find that *Meeting Wise* speaks to you. To get the most out of the book, be sure to set aside some time to do the "Try It Yourself" activities that are embedded within each chapter. These explorations are designed to ensure that you don't just take our word for it, but that you test the ideas we offer and decide which of them ring true in your context.

Before you start, we encourage you to find a "meeting buddy" so that you have someone with whom to trade insights and wonderings. For the most powerful results, however, consider having *everyone* on your team or in your organization read the book together. With a critical mass of people thinking critically and creatively about how to remake collaborative time, imagine what changes you can produce—not just in meetings, but in the culture of how people work and learn together.

While we encourage you to read the book one time all the way through, we have also designed it so that you can easily dip back into particular sections later as questions, dilemmas, and new situations arise.

We wrote this book to get a conversation started. As you make your own discoveries, please share them with your colleagues and with us at http://www.gse.harvard.edu/meetingwise. We have no doubt that the key to using meetings as a powerful lever for improving learning for all students lies not in these pages, but in the collective wisdom and actions of those who read them.

SECTION I   THINKING DIFFERENTLY

1

WHY FOCUS ON MEETINGS?

IMAGINE THAT YOU ARE looking forward to every meeting on your calendar for the next week. When you get to each meeting, you engage deeply with colleagues as you make meaningful progress toward a shared goal. You leave energized and purposeful, thinking or acting differently. How much imagination does that take? If your meetings life is anything like ours, it takes more imagination for some meetings than others.

The first step in reimagining meetings is thinking about them differently—thinking about them less as obligation and more as opportunity; less as waste and more as precious resource. Think about meetings as a place for active learning, not sitting and getting.

TIME AS A RESOURCE

When we ask people what gets in the way of improving learning and teaching, "time" is consistently one of the top three responses. Specifically, not enough time. We feel that same pinch of time and that same wistful "If we just had more time, we could . . ." We often wish for a mythical day between Tuesday and Wednesday or the ability to bend the space-time continuum like the characters in Madeleine L'Engle's *A Wrinkle in Time*. However, we haven't found a tesseract yet, and so we start with the time we have.

Time—especially time for adults to learn together—is a precious resource, and in lots of schools and conference rooms, time is being wasted. While the research base on the use of time is not deep, one finding is clear: *quality matters more than quantity*. This is not to say that quantity doesn't matter. It does, and you need a baseline amount of time in order to do high-quality work and learning. What that amount is will depend on context and what kind of work and learning is required. Fifteen minutes once a week, which is what teachers have in one school Liz visited, is not going to be enough for deep learning, no matter how strategically those fifteen minutes are used. In most situations, though, the important question is not "Do we have enough time?" but "Are we making the best use of the time we already have?"

Our colleague Richard Elmore refers to time as "money you've already spent," which acknowledges that when you're paying people salaries, you're essentially paying them for their time. If you think about a meeting not as "60 minutes," but as "$1,000" (for example, 25 people × 1 hour × $40/hour), all of a sudden the meeting feels a little different. Use the activity in "Try It Yourself: Estimate the Cost of Meetings" to see how time converts to money in your organization.

Chances are, the number that you calculated is higher than you might have expected. And that number doesn't even include preparation time! Making a big investment in meetings makes sense—*if* the time is well spent. But is it? Use the activity in "Try It Yourself: Rate the Quality of Your Meetings" to capture your perceptions.

If all of your meetings are an excellent use of time, congratulations! We would love to hear how you do it and learn from your strategies. If, on the other hand, you have a substantial fraction of time that you tolerate or waste, don't despair. Just by recognizing that there is room for improvement, you have taken the first step toward investing that time more effectively.

What would you say if we told you that you've got $100,000 earning little to no interest, and there's a way to invest that money that will pay big dividends for learning? You might be properly cautious and reply that you're not buying whatever we're selling. But we're not selling anything. We're inviting you to reimagine and reinvest a resource you and your colleagues already possess: your time together. Whenever you have people rolling their eyes or tearing their hair out at the prospect of another meeting, watching the clock as a meeting drags on, or resenting a meeting for the "real" work that it displaces,

✎ Try It Yourself
Estimate the Cost of Meetings

1. Think of a regular meeting you attend. Estimate the cost of that meeting in a year (multiply the number of *people* at the meeting by the number of *hours* in the meeting by the average *hourly earnings* of the people in the meeting by the number of *meetings per year*). What is the annual investment in that meeting?

    ____ people × ____ hours × ____ hourly earnings × ____ meetings per year = $ _____ /year

2. Estimate the cost of *all* the meetings in your organization.

Meeting *type*	**A.** Number of *people* at this type of meeting	**B.** Number of *hours* this meeting lasts	**C.** *Average hourly earnings* of participants	**D.** *Number of meetings* per year	**E.** *Cost* of meeting per year (AxBxCxD)
Total annual investment in all meetings per year					

something is wrong. Our experience is that many organizations have at least $100,000 worth of people hours (and often many orders of magnitude more) being underutilized in any given year. In fact, many school systems will spend at least that much in a single *day* of professional development.

Try It Yourself
Rate the Quality of Your Meetings

Using the circle below, create a pie chart that captures your perception of the percentage of meetings that *you* attend in your organization that are an excellent use of time, a tolerable use of time, and a waste of time.

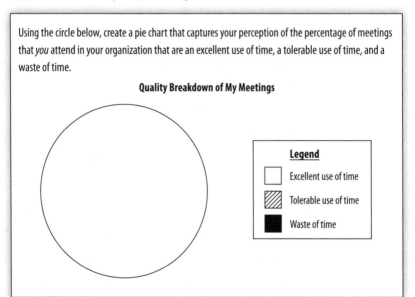

MEETINGS AS POWERFUL LEARNING SPACES

Children everywhere need challenging, nurturing learning environments that allow them to grow into thoughtful adults who can thrive in a changing world. Creating and sustaining those environments is the task of a host of adults within and beyond the education sector, including parents, teachers, coaches, principals, administrators, superintendents, school board members, policy makers, community and business leaders, and elected officials. Improvement in student achievement—and most other outcomes worth caring about—depends critically on whether these adults can continually and productively learn together.

Building a Learning Organization

The term "learning organization" is used in the business world to describe an institution that routinely gathers a broad range of data on its own activities, interprets the data collectively, and then acts deliberately to get better at what it does. By systematically identifying and sharing areas for improvement and effective practices as they evolve, learning organizations ensure that they will continue to thrive, even as the individuals working within their ranks might come and go.

In *Schools That Learn: A Fifth Discipline Handbook for Educators, Parents, and Everyone Who Cares About Education*, Peter Senge and coauthors make a strong case that *schools* can and should become learning organizations.[1] It may seem obvious that organizations whose primary focus is learning need to be places of rich and pervasive learning for everyone in the organization. Historically, however, education has been more focused on student learning that doesn't require much adult or organizational learning. That works fine if you're willing to settle for *some* children learning, or for most students doing routine tasks that demand little of their brains (the kind of tasks that used to pay decently well in the workforce and are now largely done by computers). That approach also works if you're asking adults to do things they already know how to do. But if you're trying to educate *all* students well, then adults need to learn how to address complex, unprecedented challenges, and they need to be in organizations that support that learning. In order to fulfill the mission of educating all students well, *every* organization in the education sector needs to engage in continuous improvement and thoughtful adaptation to changing circumstances.

Writing in the *Harvard Business Review*, David Garvin, Amy Edmondson, and Francesca Gino identify three building blocks for learning organizations: (1) a supportive learning environment, (2) concrete learning processes and practices, and (3) leadership behavior that reinforces learning.[2] In this book, we shine a bright light on the second of these building blocks, arguing that one of the most powerful practices in support of organizational learning is consistently having great meetings. But that begs the question: what makes a meeting great? Before we dive into our take on meetings, we invite you to reflect on your own personal experience (see "Try It Yourself: Describe Terrible and Great Meetings).

We have asked these questions of hundreds of educators over the years, and we have been amazed to see the consistency across responses—and how closely their answers mirror ours. Terrible meetings are suffocating. They make people feel bored, frustrated, and sometimes downright angry. If there is an agenda, it's not followed, or it's hijacked—and that's tolerated. Meetings run long, and everyone

Try It Yourself
Describe Terrible and Great Meetings

---

1. List the three worst meetings (or series of meetings) you have ever been in:

   a. _____

   b. _____

   c. _____

2. Take exactly two minutes to write down everything you can think of that made those meetings so terrible.

   _____

   _____

3. List the three best meetings (or series of meetings) you have ever been in:

   a. _____

   b. _____

   c. _____

4. Take another two minutes to write down everything you can think of that made those meetings so great.

   _____

   _____

---

complains afterward—but not to the people in charge of the meetings. There are side conversations or people checking e-mail or doing other tasks on the sly (or openly, which can be worse!). During bad meetings, participants' minds are consumed by endless chatter: Did we really need a meeting to cover this? Is she really going to make that same point she always makes *again*? Are we really going to pretend that what we decide here matters? Is it possible that my watch has stopped?

On the flip side, great meetings are invigorating. The purpose is clear, and achieving it is important to everyone involved. There is an agenda, often set with collaborative input, and the group moves through the agenda—not too fast and not too slow, adjusting as needed, with purpose in mind. Everyone participates in and contributes to the meeting. Even when the work itself is extremely challenging, in a great meeting there are often some number of minutes during which the group is in a state of "flow," experiencing a timelessness that brings deep creativity and connection.[3] And, at the most basic level, *great meetings are fun.*

Great Meetings Are Like Great Classrooms

If every meeting is a potentially rich opportunity for adult learning, then it makes sense that great meetings have a lot in common with great classrooms. In both, participants are actively engaged in challenging tasks, using their minds, solving problems, and communicating. In meetings, the facilitator is like a skillful teacher who plays different kinds of roles, sharing the work and meaning-making with the participants the way teachers actively engage students. And in both, all participants know the norms of behavior that they are expected to follow, and each encounter is set up to help reinforce those norms.

A meeting agenda lays out the facilitator's map for how a group will use a particular meeting to take a few steps toward a shared but often distant goal. This is analogous to the way an individual lesson plan helps students take one step of many toward desired outcomes, like building the knowledge and skills needed for mastery.

Wise facilitators uses agendas not as a straitjackets but as guides to be adapted as needs arise, just as teachers often adjust their lesson plans in the moment to take into account circumstances as they unfold.

The analogy holds up to this point, but then breaks down at a critical place. Before becoming certified to lead a classroom, most teachers take courses on how to develop good lesson plans, and work with mentors to learn how to execute and adjust those plans with real students. But where is the training and mentorship on how to develop a solid agenda and use it to run a good meeting? Where is the guidance on how to skillfully participate in a meeting, bringing your full self to the task at hand?

To Meet or Not to Meet

As you become increasingly conscious of the value of collaborative time, you may discover an interesting phenomenon: *many meetings include tasks that do not necessarily require collaborative time to do.* Finding out about a new policy or hearing schoolwide results of the latest high-stakes assessment are not *necessarily* dependent on or even enhanced by being done in a group. Yet in meetings at every level of the education system and in every country, valuable meeting time is being spent on these activities. Why?

The most common argument is that well-meaning educators are extremely busy people who would not be able to find the time outside of meetings to do these activities, so it makes sense to set aside time in everyone's calendar to be sure they happen. An alternative argument is that the people who call meetings do not always take the time to think critically about which of their agenda items require collaborative time and which could be better done independently.

For the purposes of this book, we define an effective meeting as one that helps a group of people make progress on objectives that are in explicit service of the broader goal of *improving the core work of the educational enterprise: learning and teaching.* If you are tempted to protest that some meetings "just have to happen" and aren't about improvement, we invite you to think about whether you found the description of a learning organization earlier in this chapter appealing. If you did, the question becomes whether you have ample time for engaging in that kind of continuous improvement. Most educational organizations we know feel short on time for improving learning and teaching. If time is a limited resource for you, spend it wisely.

In meetings that are truly in the service of improvement, either learning needs to be taking place in the meeting, or it must be made clear how the meeting connects to learning. Examples include an intervention team working with a parent to design a student support plan, a teacher team looking at student work to assess the effectiveness of a lesson, an operations team figuring out how to make the buses run on time, or a district team discussing how to make rich out-of-school experiences widely available. In each case, to make real progress, adults need to think or act differently, and it's easy to draw a line from the purpose of the meeting to improving learning.

If the connection between a meeting and learning is not immediately obvious, it's worth asking if a meeting is even needed in the first place. In this world of instant information sharing, could the business be addressed in another way? After all, not everything warrants a meeting!

Or, if the information is so important, why not figure out a way to use the meeting time to make sure everyone *knows* it, and is not just *told* it? How about including a quiz with polling clickers? Or having meeting participants teach one another? Or giving small groups an opportunity to apply the knowledge to their daily work?

When people will sit through a meeting in which they're being talked at for more than thirty minutes and not protest at all, that's evidence that there's a culture of acceptance of meetings as endurance activities rather than learning opportunities. If you can't tell a compelling story that explains why spending precious time convening a group of adults on a particular issue will ultimately serve learning and teaching, don't meet. Or if you do meet, change the meeting experience.

2

THE MEETING WISE CHECKLIST

YOU KNOW A GREAT meeting when you see one. And you probably know many of the big and little things you can do when planning a meeting to increase the chances that it will be successful. Yet have you ever noticed how easy it is to forget at least one of the things *as you plan*, and then forget a handful more *as the meeting unfolds*?

We sure have. And the more we thought about it, the more puzzled we were by our own behavior. Making a meeting agenda just wasn't that hard. So why didn't we get it right every time?

Atul Gawande's *The Checklist Manifesto* offered an answer to our question. From operating rooms to airplane cockpits, Gawande explains, professionals rely on checklists to remind themselves of the "minimum necessary steps" needed in a particular situation.[1] Intensive care nurses make sure they use checklists to keep patients from developing infections or taking the wrong medication. Pilots use checklists to make sure that they don't leave the runway until they are truly cleared for takeoff. Construction engineers use checklists to make sure the skyscrapers they build will remain standing. Gawande provides a host of examples of how, around the world, checklists save lives by making sure nothing obvious and routine is forgotten and freeing up professionals to focus their energy on the unique challenges of a particular situation.

With this idea in mind, we got to work. If we could identify those minimum steps for making a good meeting agenda, maybe a checklist could save us—and others—from committing the educational equivalent of leaving a sponge inside a patient.

For the last several years, we have worked with educators from across the education sector to identify the most important things to consider when planning a meeting. The result is the Meeting Wise Checklist (see Exhibit 2.1), which contains 12 questions to make sure you have all the ingredients for a successful meeting.

The questions on the checklist are grouped into categories that capture the four aspects of any meeting: *purpose, process, preparation,* and *pacing.* This chapter provides a close look at each question individually; chapter 3 then explores how to use the checklist as a whole to rethink your approach to meetings.

Exhibit 2.1

The Meeting Wise Checklist		YES	NO
PURPOSE	**1.** Have we identified clear and important meeting **objectives** that contribute to the goal of improving learning?	☐	☐
	2. Have we established the **connection** between the work of this and other meetings in the series?	☐	☐
PROCESS	**3.** Have we incorporated **feedback** from previous meetings?	☐	☐
	4. Have we chosen challenging **activities** that advance the meeting objectives and engage all participants?	☐	☐
	5. Have we assigned **roles**, including facilitator, timekeeper, and note taker?	☐	☐
	6. Have we built in time to identify and commit to **next steps**?	☐	☐
	7. Have we built in time for **assessment** of what worked and what didn't in the meeting?	☐	☐
PREPARATION	**8.** Have we gathered or developed **materials** (drafts, charts, etc.) that will help to focus and advance the meeting objectives?	☐	☐
	9. Have we determined what, if any, **pre-work** we will ask participants to do before the meeting?	☐	☐
PACING	**10.** Have we put **time allocations** to each activity on the agenda?	☐	☐
	11. Have we ensured that we will address the **primary objective** early in the meeting?	☐	☐
	12. Is it **realistic** that we could get through our agenda in the time allocated?	☐	☐

PURPOSE

The single most effective thing you can do to have a good meeting is to get crystal clear about *why* you are meeting and what you hope to accomplish. You've seen for yourself that meeting time is a precious resource. So before spending any of that treasure, think deeply about exactly what you are hoping to achieve in the meeting at hand and how that connects to all the other times the group will be working together.

Question 1: Have we identified clear and important meeting *objectives* that contribute to the goal of improving learning?

It is no accident that this is the first question on the checklist. If you can't answer "yes" to this question, don't bother moving on to the others! Give yourself the time and space to think through your objectives. Or better yet, find a critical friend who can think with you about what the meeting is all about. You may want to start by nailing down what *kind* of meeting you are planning. Is the goal to brainstorm? To decide? To produce something tangible? To get to know one another so that you can work together effectively in the coming year?

Once you know what your objectives are, showcase them at the top of your agenda. We like to start each of our meeting objectives with a strong verb. To build a sense of shared ownership among meeting participants, we try using verbs that reflect the perspective of the meeting participants, not our perspective as facilitators. So, if you've called a meeting to *get feedback* on a lesson plan you wrote, the objective from the participants' perspective would be "*provide feedback* on draft lesson plan." Other examples of clear and important objectives from a variety of meetings include:

- *Learn* what the new schoolwide policy for accepting students into advanced placement courses is and *analyze* how it affects our department's assessment strategy.

- *Develop* a shared understanding of how special education students are performing in mathematics statewide.

- *Know* how to use the new website to schedule parent/teacher conferences and access your child's data portfolio.

- *Build* community through understanding why each team member chose a career in education.

Note that question 1 specifically mentions that the meeting's objectives "contribute to the goal of improving learning." As we discussed in chapter 1, we broadly define *learning* to include the experience not just of children, but also of the millions of adults who directly or indirectly affect them. Thus, it is important to be able to draw a line between what will happen in the meeting and the improved learning of children and adults.

One thing to keep an eye on when crafting objectives is the extent to which your objectives focus on imparting information. In the first objective listed above, the meeting participants (in this case, a high school social studies department) will not just learn *what* the new placement policy is. They will also create new shared knowledge about *how* the policy could or should affect their assessment approach. For strictly informational objectives, try adding an extra kicker that dials up the rigor of the objective and challenges participants to do something with the information they are learning.

In the second objective on the list, although adults' developing an understanding of special education students' performance in math will not in and of itself increase learning, it is easy to tell a story that links this understanding to better math instruction and improved student learning.

But what if the link is not so direct? Many educators have told us that their meetings do not typically have written objectives, and that the unwritten ones (planning events, venting about difficult people, reacting to discipline issues) are not particularly strategic uses of scarce collaborative time. Admittedly, there are lots of occasions when groups need to do things that are tenuously related to learning. That's life, and that's okay—within reason. Taking a few minutes at the beginning of a staff meeting to "decide how to honor Pat's retirement" may help foster the kind of caring community that allows learning to flourish, and therefore be justified. But allowing that discussion to become the primary focus of an entire meeting *that is supposed to be in service of improving learning and teaching* isn't.

Question 2: Have we established the *connection* between the work of this and other meetings in the series?

As you think about the objectives of a particular meeting, locate that meeting within the ongoing work of the group over time. Take the example of a central office leadership team whose *overall* purpose was to coordinate the delivery of a world-class education to all students. The team's *summer* project was to engage in a planning process as it transitioned to a new superintendent. "Create a strategic plan" was too ambitious to be listed as an objective for any one of the team's two-hour summer meetings, however. So the team broke down the summer project into manageable chunks (see Exhibit 2.2).

Once you are clear on how the objectives of a series of meetings fit together, there are many strategies you can use to make sure meeting participants are aware of the connections. One of our favorites is opening and closing each meeting with a quick orientation to where the group is in their collective work. For example, the central office leadership team could do this with a little "You are here" marker in the appropriate place on their "Objectives of Summer Meetings" table.

However, it's not always realistic to plan the objectives of a series of meetings. This is particularly common when a group comes together with a shared goal (such as increasing the school engagement of families of English language learners) but no clear sense of how to achieve it. It is fine to evolve meeting to meeting, connecting forward rather than backward. The key is to leave space in a meeting for making the connections as they come about and, whenever possible, to have a high-level plan of attack to reassure the group that there is some direction as they embark on an ambiguous pathway.

Another way to drive home the point that meetings connect is to open each meeting by reminding people about the next steps that

Exhibit 2.2

Leadership Team: Objectives of Summer Meetings	
WEEK	MEETING OBJECTIVE
I	*Build* our leadership team by sharing who we are, what we do, and why this work matters to us
2	*Offer* perspectives and data on where we are now
3	*Create* a shared vision of where we want to be
4	*Define* who our stakeholders are and *outline* a work plan for working with them to develop a strategy to reach our vision

participants agreed to in the previous meeting and providing an update on the progress made on them. In addition to establishing a clear connection between meetings, this practice helps hold everyone accountable for doing the things they said they'd do. It helps the group track and appreciate its progress, inspires persistence through the inevitable messiness of collaborative work, and can help each individual understand his or her responsibility for moving the group ahead.

PROCESS

It is essential to be clear about *what* needs to get done at the meeting. But it is also critical to be thoughtful about *how* to engage the group in working toward the stated objectives.

Question 3: Have we incorporated *feedback* from previous meetings?

Wise meetings end by asking participants for an assessment of what aspects of the meeting's process worked well and what they would have liked to change. This feedback then informs future planning.

We like to open every meeting by showing the actual feedback that was created in the previous meeting (for meetings with just a few participants) or by showing a summary of the feedback (for meetings of large groups). Creating the summary can be tricky, because although you want to honor each person's responses, you also want to make sure the amount of information you share is manageable. For large groups, we typically show the "greatest hits" of the feedback (often providing the number of respondents associated with each item) and then make the full feedback available on our shared website (so that people who are curious can look deeper).

Consider the feedback and make reasoned decisions, then briefly explain your thinking to the group. For example, if participants tell you that they found it hard to follow along, you might plan to open the next meeting by letting people know that you hope to address this difficulty by giving everyone a copy of the presentation slides that you will be speaking from, or by doing regular checks for understanding, or both. Or suppose the feedback indicated that the meeting's focus on college-level skills felt "irrelevant" to educators in the room who work with elementary school students. You could take a number of different tacks in planning the next meeting's agenda—e.g., provide examples of those skills at multiple grade levels or dedicate time for people to turn and talk about the connections to their context. Or you could decide not to address it in the next meeting and instead explain why not. Maybe you want everyone in the room to be aware of what it takes to get into college, even if the students they serve are only recently out of diapers. Explaining your rationale can go a long way to helping people feel that their input was heard—even if not completely addressed.

Remember: you don't have to act on every suggestion, and it is not always the popularity of a response that makes it important and relevant to address in the next session. Just be clear with yourself and the group about *why* you're incorporating or not incorporating particular feedback.

Question 4: Have we chosen challenging *activities* that advance the meeting objectives and engage all participants?

When we ask teachers about the level of rigor of the work they give students, they often respond by telling us where a particular task falls among the six levels of intellectual demand described by Bloom's Taxonomy (remembering, understanding, applying, analyzing, evaluating, and creating).[2]

Teachers are proud when their lesson plans call for high-rigor activities because they believe these activities are more powerful for learning than those that require students to "sit and get." Well, guess what? The same is true for adults. If you approach each meeting as an opportunity for rich adult learning, you will be thinking critically about the tasks that will best support the learning experience.

For a given meeting objective, you may have a wider range of options than you realize. For example, if the objective for a meeting with families is for participants to "know how to use the new website to schedule parent/teacher conferences and access your child's data portfolio," a typical approach might be create an instruction handout for parents, project it on a screen at the front of the room, and walk parents through the steps. This could be followed by a lighthearted pop quiz at the end, encouraging people to *remember* what they have learned.

Alternatively, an activity could be planned that focuses more on providing an opportunity for parents to *understand* how and why they might want to use the new system. They could be put into groups and asked to share their ideas around why it could be important to have regular communication with teachers and how and when they could see themselves using the new system. Even better, though, might be allowing parents to *apply* their learning. Students could teach their parents how to log on to school computers or their smartphones during the meeting. Think about how immediate the learning could be if parents tackled the task of tracking down a particular assessment report on the spot, and then scheduled their first conference before they had even left the meeting! If you go this route, you may even find you want to reconsider how you phrase the objective. Instead of aiming to have participants simply know how to use the new website, you may want to reword things so that the goal is to practice actually using the system.

So far we've focused on the "challenging activities" part of question 4. But this question also invites you to reflect on the extent to which the meeting activities you are planning will "engage all participants." When there are only two or three people in a meeting, a simple conversation may be all that is needed. However, in larger groups, you may want to structure the conversation so that no one can opt out of participating in the work of the meeting. Everyone has strengths, and it is worth thinking about how to set things up so that you tap into them.

Our go-to strategy for meaningfully engaging participants is using discussion "protocols." Protocols are like a blueprint for a discussion; they provide structure to conversations through prompts and clarification of when individuals are expected to speak—and when they need to listen. Protocols can involve time to reflect silently, work with a partner, or address the group as a whole.

If you are new to protocols but intrigued by the concept, please see Selected Protocols at the end of this book. There we point you to several online and print resources that can get you started using these powerful collaborative tools and offer step-by-step instructions for facilitating a couple of our favorites. Using protocols opens up new possibilities by providing concrete strategies for addressing power dynamics and other group dynamics that could be holding some people back from active participation.

You don't always need to use a published protocol, however. As you plan the meeting, feel free to be creative. For example, in a ninety-minute conference call to design a principal network, instead of having an open discussion, you could put some structure around the conversation; for example, starting by having everyone type into a shared online document their personal vision for the network and then having participants comment on the common elements they saw across statements. That way, everyone contributes from the very beginning. You could then break up the remaining time into four shorter intervals, each dedicated to addressing a basic question about the network: What is the purpose of the network? How will it be structured? Who will join? When will members collaborate? You could conclude by having different participants offer to summarize the key points of each discussion. Breaking an open discussion into manageable chunks and broadly sharing the work of meaning making can help participants stay engaged with the work.

All this said, remember that just because you set things up so that the heart of the meeting will be devoted to a challenging task that supports learning, that doesn't mean you can't plan to use a few minutes of meeting time for logistical tasks that are most efficiently done in person. For example, if participants know to bring their calendars to the meeting, it can be very efficient to allow subgroups time to schedule their breakout meetings when everyone is the same room instead of leaving them to do that virtually, which can often take much longer.

Also, know that wise meetings are not necessarily serious ones in which every spare moment is spent in a structured activity with nose to grindstone. Feel free to build in the little things that help make a group feel like a community. Singing "Happy Birthday," sharing a slide show of an important event, starting off with a round-robin check-in to see how everyone is doing, and enjoying a meal can all be very worthwhile uses of collaborative time. After all, we are all people first, people who love to laugh and feel appreciated and connected to others. Taking time to make meetings fun often opens up the possibility that people will relax into being their best selves. And when people bring their best selves to a meeting, the chances go way up that the group will achieve its purpose.

Question 5: Have we assigned *roles*, including facilitator, timekeeper, and note taker?

Even if you plan an agenda on your own, we still heartily recommend that you think carefully about how you can involve others in actually making the meeting happen. The three main roles to consider are: facilitator, timekeeper, and note taker. You may also want to add additional roles (we offer some suggestions below) that would be useful in the context of your meeting.

Although for some recurring meetings it makes sense to assign these roles to specific individuals for the whole series, we recommend that, when possible, these roles be rotated to develop a shared sense of ownership of the work. For example, the rotation could be set early in the year or semester and posted in each meeting's agenda. In small groups, everyone might have a job at all times: for example, if someone brings snacks to one meeting, then that person is timekeeper and then note taker and then facilitator in the following meetings. In large groups, you might either invite people to sign up for roles or assign them.

The *facilitator* has a very important job: to make it easier for the participants to achieve the meeting objectives. In chapter 5, we will offer our best wisdom on *how* to do that job, but for now we will consider *who* you should assign to do it. The default in most educational settings is for meetings to be facilitated by the participant with the most positional authority. This makes some sense: as the group's leader, that person often has the power to convene the meeting and to decide how the minutes will be spent.

But that doesn't always mean that the group leader is the ideal person to lead every discussion. In fact, we have seen potent results when a leader decides to share facilitation responsibilities with others. Principals accustomed to running an entire two-hour staff meeting have told us how liberated they have felt when they began delegating facilitation of all or part of the meeting to other staff members. "I used to be like the Little Red Hen, who always said 'Very well then, I'll do it myself,'" one leader told us. "But that meant that I could never just participate. And I was doing nothing to develop the leadership capacity of others." Deciding whom to tap for facilitation responsibility can be very strategic. Will a conversation about adjusting priorities at a community college be better received if led by a faculty member than if led by an administrator? Will an impartial third party make more headway than the director in helping a school board subcommittee reach a compromise?

For smaller meetings, especially of people who see themselves as peers, rotating facilitation can be a powerful strategy. It builds a sense of empathy about what the role of facilitator involves, thus making people better participants, too. In meetings of only two or three people, it might not even make sense to have a designated facilitator, since roles will be informal and overlapping.

Another thing to consider is having two people share facilitation. Particularly when we have a meeting of more than a couple of hours, our top choice is to have a co-facilitator. It makes a tremendous difference in how nimbly we can adjust in the moment if we have another set of eyes and ears noticing what is happening and thinking about what to do next. We like to switch off which one of us leads each activity, so that the other can focus on how close we are coming to "landing" the meeting's objectives. That person can also do some quick clock math in the moment when things run over allotted time so that we know how to adjust to be able to stay on track.

The *timekeeper* is a role that we (reluctantly!) came to embrace as being extremely important. This happened as meeting after meeting that one or the other of us was facilitating ran over time. How was it that, no matter how carefully we planned a meeting, we never seemed able to keep within the minutes allowed? Turns out, the facilitator has plenty to stay on top of without managing time as well. Having one person dedicated to making everyone aware of whether or not you are on track toward a timely finish can make a tremendous difference in whether you achieve that goal.

The *note taker* is the person who will capture the events of the meeting so that you have a record of what has taken place. If you don't already have someone who is the obvious choice because of his or her role in the organization, you'll need to find a volunteer or establish a rotating schedule. Regardless, consider how being note taker might affect someone's participation and the group's perception of that person's status. On the one hand, the note taker is performing what may historically have been viewed as a menial task, and may result in having the person hold back on participation. On the other hand, he or she has the power to portray what happened in the meeting for the consumption of participants and sometimes a wider audience. Here are a few tips about this critical role:

1. **Make the note taker's job clear.** Is the note taker supposed to write down, as close to verbatim as possible, everything that is said in the meeting? Or is he or she simply to capture

decisions and next steps? Either way, when you assign the role, make sure the note taker knows it requires expert listening but not editorializing.

2. **Have a backup note taker.** After trial and error, we discovered that it is important to have a backup note taker step in whenever the official note taker speaks. This avoids giving those in the role the nearly impossible challenge of capturing their own thoughts as they speak them.

3. **Encourage people with positional authority to be note taker.** When we offer to take notes in a group where one of us holds the clear positional authority, we have been delighted to see how effectively this role keeps us from trying to put our own two cents in after every comment. Because our eyes might be down as we take notes, it also encourages others to speak to one another instead of to one of us. Finally, it helps to show how firmly we believe that improving education requires standing old hierarchies on their heads and finding ways to have leaders serve the group—instead of the other way around.

Additional roles that can be useful to assign include *next steps tracker*, someone who keeps an ear out for anything that sounds like a to-do item and helps the group be sure to capture who is going to do what by when. You may also decide to name a *process checker*, someone who focuses on noticing and documenting how group dynamics are playing out. Some groups also have a *summarizer*, who offers a synthesis (not a complete repeat!) of what has been said. Depending on what the group is working on, we sometimes will fold into this role naming questions or ideas that were introduced but not picked up by the group.

Question 6: Have we built in time to identify and commit to *next steps*?

In our experience, next steps tend to arise throughout a meeting, and we do our best to recognize them as such as they are mentioned. But it is also useful to set aside a few minutes toward the end of the meeting to summarize the next steps that have been proposed, identify who will be responsible for each one, and confirm the date by which each item will be completed.

There are situations where this relentless focus on productivity and accountability may feel off-putting or inappropriate. You can of course choose not to set aside meeting time to identify and commit to next steps provided you considered the option and *decided* that was the right thing to do. Just be aware that if you don't make time to explicitly confirm who's doing what, all the next steps could default to being left in the facilitator's lap. Developing a discipline of being explicit about next steps can help a group of colleagues evolve into a learning organization where understanding and responsibility are broadly shared.

Question 7: Have we built in time for *assessment* of what worked and what didn't in the meeting?

A tremendous opportunity arises as a meeting winds down. The people who know best about how it went are all gathered in one place, and the meeting itself is fresh in their minds. Why not plan to tap into their insights right in the moment, and then use those insights to help design an even better meeting the next time around? If you don't dedicate meeting time to doing this, it's not likely to happen on its own.

When we first introduce the Meeting Wise Checklist to educators, this question is one that they most frequently check "no." But once they realize that getting in-the-moment feedback from participants doesn't need to take more than five minutes (see, for example, the Plus/Delta Protocol in the Resources section), they often see that scheduling a few minutes to learn from experience generates rapid improvement of meeting quality.

That said, there are plenty of times when we choose not include a formal assessment of the meeting as an agenda item. In some meetings—especially small ones, or those where participants and facilitator are in different places on a clear hierarchy—asking for feedback might be just plain weird. You don't really need to ask your boss to jot down and share feedback about how a routine status meeting went, especially if *her* boss is in the room and their power dynamic might make her comments less than useful to you. And you certainly don't need to put a newly hired assistant on the spot the first day, asking for feedback on how you ran your first planning meeting before he has even had a chance to understand that's "how you roll" in the new office.

PREPARATION

Now that you've planned purpose and process, step back and consider what else the facilitator and participants could do in advance to make sure the meeting goes smoothly.

Question 8: Have we gathered or developed *materials* (drafts, charts, etc.) that will help to focus and advance the meeting objectives?

The important thing to consider when reflecting on this question is whether there is anything you can do ahead of time or bring to the meeting that will make it easier for the group to dive into the content. For almost every meeting, it is possible to anticipate some of the questions that participants are likely to raise. For example, if you are holding a meeting to address bullying in your community, you might anticipate that the group will want to know a history of bullying incidents in the schools in your area over time, actions taken to date, and ideas from other communities that are tackling this issue. Compiling this information ahead of time lays the foundation so that the group can more quickly get to a deeper conversation.

When developing materials, we remind ourselves the old adage of a picture being worth a thousand words. It is the rare participant who appreciates being handed a pile of numbers, given very little time to sort through it, and then being expected to know what the numbers mean. On the other hand, participants who are given ample time to digest clear and compelling displays of information are usually energized. The information you share is bound to raise even more questions, but this is good: if the goal of your meeting is to tap into the energy and expertise of a group, why not get to those deeper, harder questions faster? The same thing goes for text: avoid giving people lengthy documents to read during a meeting. Having the text available in advance or choosing a provocative quote or excerpt for the meeting is much more powerful.

We sometimes like to think of it as "leapfrogging": is there a way to jump over the content of the meeting *we thought we were having* and propel ourselves toward the *meeting after that*, which might be an even more exciting and productive one? When it is important to ensure that no avenue of thinking be cut off prematurely, the answer to this question can be "no." But it is certainly worth asking.

Question 9: Have we determined what, if any, *pre-work* we will ask participants to do before the meeting?

At a minimum, ask participants to prepare for the meeting by reading the agenda that you have created. If appropriate, offer that agenda as a draft, and welcome feedback by a particular date. Be sure to specify the kind of feedback you are looking for; if there are some aspects of the meeting that are nonnegotiable, it's best to state that up front so that you don't get a bunch of suggestions you are powerless or unwilling to adopt. A cover note that goes with the agenda is an opportunity to reinforce the meeting's purpose, highlight preparation, get people excited about the meeting, and invite questions.

Beyond reading the agenda, consider asking people to do other kinds of pre-work. For example, for a teacher team meeting, you could ask colleagues to bring samples of student work to ground a conversation in evidence about what students are learning. For a meeting of coach supervisors, you could ask them to have formal or informal conversations with the people they supervise about topics to inform the group's discussion. For a meeting with parents around risky behaviors of high school students, you could provide optional background reading on the topic. If the purpose of the meeting is to produce a document, you could create a "straw man" in advance of the meeting and ask people to read it for pre-work and come prepared to offer ideas for revisions.

Whenever your agenda references a document (to read as pre-work, for example), we recommend posting the document on an internal website and then embedding a link to the document directly into the agenda. This makes it easy for participants to do their homework. When documents can be accessed with a simple click, participants are more likely to follow through than when they need to deal with lengthy website addresses or crawl around through their email looking for attachments.[3]

When deciding whether to require pre-work, provide participants your best guess as to how long it will take so that people can budget their time. Also, be clear about whether an assignment is required or optional. If it is required, be sure that you plan on using it during the meeting so that people feel that the time they spent preparing was justified.

If it is unlikely that most people will do required pre-work, don't assign it (unless the group is focusing on pre-work as an area of improvement—more on that in chapter 7). When it comes time for the meeting, you'll be in the unenviable position of having to decide whether to bore those who prepared (by taking meeting time to catch the others up), or to frustrate those who did not (by forging ahead with work they might not be able to understand). It may be better to just set aside meeting time for people to silently read through a short but carefully chosen excerpt. When the two of us started doing this work, Kathy was at first hesitant to "waste" meeting time on such a silent, independent activity. Seeing how five minutes of quiet in-the-moment preparation could transform the rest of the hour, however, took care of that.

PACING

Before finalizing your agenda, dive into the details and confirm that your minutes add up and that you are spending them in the right places. Then pull back to see the big picture and ensure that you feel well poised to have the meeting you truly want to have.

Question 10: Have we put *time allocations* to each activity on the agenda?

Make sure the start time is one people can realistically do—or you're already behind before you start and you'll spend the rest of the meeting scrambling to adjust. If people are going to need to arrive over a 10-minute period owing to previous commitments, build that into the agenda, perhaps as check in time, and make it clear when the official start time is.

Participants have a right to know when a meeting is supposed to end, and a right to expect that it will indeed end on schedule. As you facilitate a meeting, you have the right to adjust in the moment to ensure that you can conclude the meeting when promised. You may decide to cut short, extend, or even eliminate an activity if you think that will best serve the meeting's purpose. But you may find that it is much easier to make these adjustments if you have put at least tentative time limits on each of your planned activities.

Parceling out the time you think each activity will take may seem nitpicky, even arbitrary. At first, we found that it was extremely difficult to accurately estimate the amount of time an activity would take, but we got better at it with experience. We started out by guessing, and then keeping track of how much we had to adjust on the fly during our meetings. Although you will doubtless discover your own truths as you experiment, here are some of the things that are true for us:

- Checking in at the beginning of a meeting to see how everyone is doing takes about 5 minutes with small groups and 10 minutes with large ones—if we're disciplined. Otherwise, it can take over the whole meeting!

- Having intervals of time on an agenda that are not multiples of five just looks weird. (12:21–12:33 for a discussion—really?)

- Participants in small meetings don't want to hear the same voice for more than 10 minutes in a row.

- Participants in large meetings (especially trainings) don't want to be talked at for more than 20 minutes.

- The amount of time allowed for "open discussion" should account for the number of people in the conversation. You need a minimum of 2–3 minutes per person. So: 5 minutes for two people, at least 10 minutes for four, etc.

- Reviewing next steps usually takes less than 5 minutes, but it is good to budget for 5, since by that point in the meeting, it is nice to have a cushion.

Question 11: Have we ensured that we will address the *primary objective* early in the meeting?

Back to objectives again? Yes! And the reason is this: as you think through the first 10 questions on the checklist, you may come to a deeper understanding of what you believe the *primary* objective of the meeting should be. This is the one objective that is most important to address in the meeting at hand. The one you will feel great about having met. The one you will feel most disappointed if you don't get to. So get to this as soon as you can.

We've tried doing it the other way: loading up the beginning of the meeting with objectives that are "easy," that we believe we can get through quickly and will therefore help build momentum that we can ride into our later objectives. Using this approach, we usually get tripped up by one of three things: (1) the easy things aren't as easy as we thought, and once we start them, we end up having to give them more time; (2) people spend their most creative energy on the easy things and are out of steam when we get to the heart of our agenda; or (3) the primary objective actually takes a lot longer than we had expected, but by doing it late in the meeting, we bump up against the hard stop of the meeting end time and have to adjourn before we have achieved our primary purpose.

If you think there is a chance you will fall into any of these pitfalls, rearrange the order of events on your agenda.

Question 12: Is it *realistic* that we could get through our agenda in the time allocated?

This final question is a gut check. Your math may add up, your primary objective may be in the perfect slot. But in your heart of hearts, do you think you can achieve what you have set out to do? If the answer is "no," we offer two choices:

- **Scale back meeting objectives that are too lofty.** "*Finalize* our plan for bringing our proposal before the state legislature" might have to be, "*Revise* our plan . . ." "*Decide* whether to change the requirements for earning graduation" may have to become "*Determine* the criteria we would use for changing . . ."

- **Toss something overboard.** Why not do so now, before you feel yourself and your crew actually going down with the ship? If you decide to shorten or eliminate an activity ahead of time, there is often nothing to stop you from including it in a future meeting when you can give it the time and space it deserves. Liz, who has a particular Achilles' heel around this checklist item, plans an agenda as tightly as she can, steps back, and then eliminates one more thing. And that usually gets her close to the right pacing. *Hint: If it feels like you're packing too much in, you are.* We have never—not once—had the sense that we were packing too much in and been wrong. But we have often—more than once or twice or twenty times—hoped that we were wrong and gone ahead with the packed agenda, only to run out of time.

One way to make sure you have a realistic agenda is to allow for at least 10 minutes of unscheduled time at the end of each meeting. We talk of it as the "kitty" or the "time bank" and appreciate it as a place to borrow time from when one of our activities runs longer than expected. The beautiful thing about having time in the bank is that it gets you off the hook of having to estimate everything precisely. When something takes longer than you guessed, it is easy to get back on track.

And if it turns out you don't need the extra time, try seeing what happens if you let people out of the meeting a few minutes early. We find this a sure way to build goodwill and trust that time will be used well.

In our own work, we have been known to spend as much *or more* time designing a meeting as actually having the meeting itself. This is owing in part to the fact that creating the agenda is not always the only thing that has to be done to prepare for a meeting (see chapter 4).

Spending so much time getting ready for a meeting struck us as odd until we reflected on how efficient it was to have *one or two* people invest a few extra hours to make sure that the hours of *everyone* at the meeting were used wisely. After all, the planning that goes into performing a successful surgery, constructing a spectacular building, or designing an exceptional science lesson is often much greater than the actual amount of time it takes to do it. Why should the planning that goes into supporting adults in working together be any different?

Try It Yourself
Use the Checklist to Review Agendas

1. Collect three agendas from meetings you have led or attended. For each agenda, write one or two sentences at the bottom describing the extent to which the meeting's purpose was accomplished.
2. Print out one copy of the Meeting Wise Checklist for each agenda and fill out a separate checklist for each agenda.
3. Array the completed checklists in front of you. What patterns do you notice? What surprises you? How do the patterns relate to the sentence you wrote at the bottom of each agenda about the extent to which the meeting's purpose was accomplished?
4. Talk with your meeting buddy about your respective assessments and patterns.

3

USING THE CHECKLIST

CHECKLISTS ARE ONLY VALUABLE if you *use* them. So how do you move from checking boxes to actually improving your agendas? Remember that the goal is not to check "yes" for every item on the Meeting Wise Checklist, but to develop meetings that make a more deliberate and successful contribution to improving learning and teaching.

To demonstrate how the checklist can be used, this chapter shows six different meeting agendas and how educators might use the checklist to improve them. The agendas vary in terms of purpose, number of participants, frequency of meeting, and nature of the power dynamic between participants, but are typical of the range of meetings and issues that people find themselves in.

In the first example, the meeting planners opt for a complete agenda overhaul, making revisions in response to nearly all of the 12 questions on the checklist. The other five examples show how the checklist can be used more as a touchstone, where the facilitators pick a few things to revise that will help address a particular pattern from which they hope to break free. The educators responsible for these agendas have decided to target something quite specific, and their agenda revisions result more from reflecting on the checklist categories—purpose, process, preparation, and pacing—than on addressing each of the 12 questions directly.

As you read this chapter, think about the patterns in your own agendas that you noticed at the end of chapter 2 when you decided to "try it yourself." We recommend that you focus not so much on who the people are in each example, but on what elements of their meetings are impeding their success and how they try to improve those elements. While many of the individuals in the examples will be in different roles from you, we expect many of their habits and struggles will feel familiar.

COMPLETE AGENDA OVERHAUL: GREENVILLE FIFTH-GRADE TEAM

■ **Teacher leader Rose Hawkins facilitates** a meeting of her fellow fifth-grade teachers at Greenville Elementary School for an hour after student dismissal every other Tuesday. The team is charged with working collaboratively to improve instruction. The five members enjoy a warm collegial culture despite the fact that there is always some teacher turnover from one year to the next. However, Rose has been feeling growing frustration among the team about the fact that meetings never end on time or with a sense of accomplishment. This was particularly true at the last meeting, where four out of five teachers stayed a full 30 minutes late—and they still left important work undone. The agenda she drafted for the next meeting is shown in Exhibit 3.1.

When Rose reviewed this draft against the Meeting Wise Checklist, she was a bit dismayed. She had always prided herself on actually *having* an agenda for all of her meetings—plenty of the other team leaders in

Exhibit 3.1

DRAFT Agenda
Greenville School Fifth-Grade Team Meeting

AGENDA FOR MARCH 4

1. Museum Field Trip
   • Permissions and chaperones
   • Imagery activity
2. State Testing
   • Goals
   • Make-up policy
   • Spring schedule
3. April Writing Prompt
   • Data review
   • Implications for instruction
4. Next Steps

Greenville Elementary School didn't bother with them. But she hadn't thought much about whether she was *leveraging* the agenda as a tool for making meetings as effective as they could be. When she compared her agenda to the checklist, she could only check "yes" to one question (see Exhibit 3.2).

She found herself wondering if her meetings would go a lot better with clear priorities and explicit connection between meetings, as well as set times for engaging in activities and distributed responsibility for keeping the meeting on track. A complete agenda makeover was in

Exhibit 3.2

Checklist for DRAFT Agenda Greenville School Fifth-Grade Team Meeting		YES	NO
PURPOSE	1. Have we identified clear and important meeting *objectives* that contribute to the goal of improving learning?	☐	☑
	2. Have we established the *connection* between the work of this and other meetings in the series?	☐	☑
PROCESS	3. Have we incorporated *feedback* from previous meetings?	☐	☑
	4. Have we chosen challenging *activities* that advance the meeting objectives and engage all participants?	☐	☑
	5. Have we assigned *roles*, including facilitator, timekeeper, and note taker?	☐	☑
	6. Have we built in time to identify and commit to *next steps*?	☑	☐
	7. Have we built in time for *assessment* of what worked and what didn't in the meeting?	☐	☑
PREPARATION	8. Have we gathered or developed *materials* (drafts, charts, etc.) that will help to focus and advance the meeting objectives?	☐	☑
	9. Have we determined what, if any, *pre-work* we will ask participants to do before the meeting?	☐	☑
PACING	10. Have we put *time allocations* to each activity on the agenda?	☐	☑
	11. Have we ensured that we will address the *primary objective* early in the meeting?	☐	☑
	12. Is it *realistic* that we could get through our agenda in the time allocated?	☐	☑

order, she decided, but she didn't want to do it alone. So she reached out to fellow fifth-grade teacher Manuel Dixon, who had excused himself at the scheduled end time of the last meeting so he wouldn't be late picking up his son. She asked if he'd be willing to work with her on using the Meeting Wise Checklist to join her in planning the next meeting, which she told him she was determined to start and end right on time. Manuel told her he'd be happy to help.

Purpose

The first thing Rose and Manuel noticed as they sat down with the checklist was that the agenda did not state objectives. Sure, there was a list of topics. But what exactly was the team expected to *accomplish* during the meeting? They decided to brainstorm a list of objectives, starting each with a verb to make sure the objective clarified what the team would do. This is the list they came up with:

POSSIBLE OBJECTIVES FOR NEXT MEETING

Field Trip
- Determine which students lack field trip permission forms
- Figure out if we have enough chaperones for the field trip
- Provide feedback on the imagery activity that students will do on the field trip

State Test
- Review district performance goals for fifth-graders
- Make sure everyone has the testing schedule and knows about the new policy for administering make-up exams

Writing Prompt
- Analyze student responses to the February writing prompt to assess how our action plan for improving student writing is going
- Decide how to adjust our writing instruction in light of what we learn from student responses.

Nine objectives in 60 minutes . . . Rose and Manuel saw right away that if they kept to this list, they'd be setting the team up for yet another extra-innings experience. But when Manuel asked Rose which of the objectives she thought it was most essential to *have the whole team work on collaboratively*, she realized that the nine weren't equally important.

Reminding themselves that the fifth-grade team's charge was to use their team time to improve instruction, they narrowed the list to

(1) providing feedback on the field trip activity, (2) analyzing student writing responses to assess how the action plan was going, and (3) deciding how to adjust instruction. Of these, the last two were especially critical; the team had made a big push to improve writing instruction over the winter, but had not made the time to assess how it was working. If they let yet another week go by without looking at some data, the action plan they had worked so hard to implement ran the risk of ending up as a fizzled experiment.

This made Rose think about the extent to which the upcoming week's meeting was connected to all the other Tuesday meetings they had had over the year—and would have throughout the spring. She had never really sketched out how their scheduled times coincided with their inquiry cycles. So she and Manuel created a table that captured all of the remaining Tuesdays in the year and how they might spend them (see Exhibit 3.3).

Exhibit 3.3

Objectives of Spring Meetings Greenville Fifth-Grade Team	
DATE	MEETING OBJECTIVE
Mar. 4	ANALYZE February writing prompt responses DECIDE how to adjust writing action plan
Mar. 18	OBSERVE adjusted writing instruction DISCUSS focus area for next inquiry cycle
Apr. 1	ANALYZE formative assessment data IDENTIFY a learner-centered problem
Apr. 15	SPRING BREAK
Apr. 29	OBSERVE instruction for clues about learner-centered problem IDENTIFY a problem of practice
May 13	DEVELOP an action plan DEVELOP a plan to assess progress
May 27	ASSESS implementation of the action plan and student data DECIDE how to adjust action plan
June 10	CELEBRATE success! PLAN for next year

Seeing the year mapped out in this way, Rose and Manuel realized the team would have its hands full just trying to get through the objectives around its inquiry work. As for all the other things they usually tried to do in their meetings, did they *really* have to happen on Tuesday afternoons? Some could be addressed through e-mail, some could be delegated to the classroom assistant who worked part-time for the grade level, and the others, well . . . Rose would need to talk with other grade-level leaders about how they dealt with the conflicting demands on collaborative meeting time.

Process

Rose and Manuel thought long and hard about the questions listed in the Process category of the checklist. They knew they wanted to start and end the meeting with a few brief "bookend" activities that would transition their colleagues into the meeting and help put the meeting in context. At the beginning of the meeting, they figured the group would need to say hello, take a deep breath, and check in about how everyone was doing. Then they decided to give the group time to review a list of the comments Rose had heard people had make on their way out the door of the last meeting. By capturing this informal feedback in writing, giving their colleagues time to digest it, and explaining how they hoped the new agenda would address their concerns, Rose and Manuel hoped to set the stage for the new way of doing business.

They also wanted to open by connecting the March 4 meeting to previous work. Rose had always ended her meetings by clarifying next steps, but it hadn't occurred to her to set aside time at the beginning of the meeting to see if the promised tasks had actually been done. She added a section to the agenda that showed the previous meeting's steps, and used a strikethrough font to show which of them had actually been completed. Doing this made Rose instantly feel more accountable to the group for the promises *she* had made; she guessed the others would feel the same.

Then Rose and Manuel talked about which activities would best support their main objectives. Manuel mentioned that when the team had used a Looking at Student Work Protocol last year, they had noticed that it had pushed them to having much more meaningful conversations about student learning than they usually did.[1] Rose agreed, and explained that because the protocol required at least a half an hour to do well, she hadn't tried to squeeze it into recent meetings. With a narrowed list of priorities, however, they decided they could take the time they needed to really dig into the writing they had asked their students to do. Also, they discussed how they would need to put some structure on their conversations. Teacher Sheryl Jensen had joined the team only recently, and she seemed unsure of how and when to come into the conversation. They hoped the protocol, which required each person to speak in turn, would give her the space to contribute.

As for finalizing the focusing activity for the big fifth-grade field trip, they decided that could be handled by setting aside a limited amount of time for a quick go-round where teachers could weigh in with their thoughts about the assignment one of the teachers had drafted.

They left time at the end of the meeting to review next steps and remind their colleagues that at the beginning of all future meetings, they would be returning to the list to see what progress had been made. They planned to finish the session with a Plus/Delta Protocol (see Selected Protocols at the end of this book) to allow the team to formally capture meeting feedback. Rose wanted the team to understand that they would have a central role in figuring out how they could continue to refine the way they used collaborative time.

Regarding roles, Rose's instinct had always been to avoid asking too much of her colleagues. She knew they were all busy people, and as team leader she didn't mind functioning as a jack-of-all-trades. But then she thought about how hard it was to facilitate a discussion while keeping a panicked eye on the clock and jotting down notes whenever she thought of it. The fact was that, with her attention split so many ways, she ended up doing none of these roles particularly well. So when Manuel offered to take notes at the next meeting, she took him up on it. And they both knew just who to tap as time keeper—Ingrid would relish the task of playing the heavy and keeping the group on pace.

Preparation

Manuel had some ideas for what they could do ahead of time to help the group makes the most of its time together. First of all, they could distribute the agenda a week in advance, handing it to their colleagues in person and explaining how they hoped the group would be willing to test out a new approach to meetings. They would ask for feedback by Friday, and then e-email the revised agenda before the end of the day on Monday.

Rose agreed to track down the instructions for the Looking at Student Work Protocol, modify them to meet her team's needs, and attach them to the agenda. Manuel suggested that the meeting would be much more productive if everyone had read the their own students' writing prompts ahead of time and came with a high, medium, and low response to discuss with the group. Rose had never asked her busy colleagues to do pre-work for team meetings, but Manuel convinced her that sufficient advance warning—combined with the fact that eventually everyone was going to have to read the writing responses for their class anyway—justified the request.

Pacing

Rose and Manuel assigned all of the meeting activities a time limit, and were disappointed to see that they had spent 10 minutes more than they actually had. They had devoted a full 20 minutes to what they had hoped would be mere opening and closing "bookends." Rose suggested shaving time from these activities, but Manuel pointed out that setting up and closing down the meeting more thoughtfully would take time; counting on saving minutes there was just wishful thinking, especially as they were just starting to take a new approach to meetings.

If they were really going to finish by 4:00 p.m., he reasoned, they would just have to cut out the 10-minute discussion about the field trip activity. They did not absolutely have to have everyone in the same room for that. Manuel pointed out that he and Ingrid had already drafted the activity, and that getting feedback on the draft could be something they could assign as pre-work.

So they removed the field trip discussion from the agenda and took a step back. They were down to question 12, the last question on the checklist. Was it realistic that the team could get through this agenda in one hour? They thought so, but agreed that when they distributed the agenda for feedback (Exhibit 3.4), they would ask their colleagues to think about this question. In fact, they decided to attach a clean copy of the Meeting Wise Checklist to the draft and invite people to refer to it as they reviewed the agenda.

As you can see, the revised agenda is more detailed than the original draft, especially with regard to connecting the March 4 meeting to

Exhibit 3.4

REVISED Agenda Greenville School Fifth-Grade Team Meeting	
MEETING AGENDA March 4, 3:00–4:00 p.m.	
TOPIC: February Writing Prompt	**Attendees:** Greenville fifth-grade team **Facilitator:** Rose **Note taker:** Manuel **Time keeper:** Ingrid
MEETING OBJECTIVES: • Analyze student responses to the February writing prompt to assess how our action plan for improving student writing is going • Decide how to adjust our writing instruction	
TO PREPARE FOR THIS MEETING, PLEASE: • Read your student's writing responses and bring a "typical" high, medium, and low writing prompt response to share with the team (2 hours) • Review the draft field trip activity and e-mail Ingrid with suggestions for revision (15 minutes)	

Schedule [60 minutes]

TIME	MINUTES	ACTIVITY
3:00–3:05	5	• Check-in and review objectives of this meeting and how they connect to future objectives
3:05–3:10	5	Review informal feedback from February 18 meeting • We started and ended late . . . again! • We didn't review the Feb. writing prompt data Review next steps from February 18 meeting • ~~By Feb. 25, Rose will incorporate today's writing prompt revisions into a final version~~ • ~~By Feb. 21, Ingrid will draft an imagery activity for the museum trip~~ • By Mar. 2, Pat will e-mail other rubric samples
3:10–3:40	30	Analyze student responses to the February writing prompt using the Looking at Student Work Protocol
3:40–3:50	10	Open discussion: decide how to adjust our writing instruction
3:50–3:55	5	Review next steps • Do we need further time to discuss adjusting our instruction?
3:55–4:00	5	Assess what worked well about this meeting and what we would have liked to change

Plus	Delta
•	•

the team's ongoing work. (Note that the revised agenda is based on the Meeting Wise Agenda Template, which is available in the Resources section of this book.) Working to instill some discipline into their meeting planning, Rose and Manuel took the lead in helping the team break free of the negative pattern they had fallen into, while keeping in mind the reality of their own and their colleagues' lives. They wanted meetings to be something that helped the whole team with the real work of student learning, not something that felt like an interruption of lesson planning, assessing papers, getting materials ready for the next day, calling parents—and all the other things that they did after working directly with students all day. They hoped that these first steps toward a more purposeful and focused meeting would help their team experience success in the time available. They also knew that one meeting wasn't going to be enough for them to change their less productive meeting patterns. For lasting change to occur, they needed to make space for everyone on the team to contribute to developing a new way of working.

* * *

This example focused on a team dynamic in which everyone knew and liked each other and no one on the team had formal supervisory role over anyone else. In the next example, we will look at a team with clear reporting relationships and weak or competitive ties between members.

TARGETING INTENTIONAL COLLABORATION: JACKSON COUNTY CENTRAL OFFICE LEADERSHIP TEAM

The Jackson County Public Schools central office leadership team had moved heaven and earth to give teachers collaborative meeting time every week. But when they saw how inefficiently the time was actually being used in schools, they were disappointed. The meetings they observed lacked focus and structure, and there was wide variation in how invested different teachers seemed in the work at hand. The leadership team decided to offer schools the Meeting Wise Checklist as a reflective tool that they hoped would lead to more productive collaboration at the school level. And even though they felt pretty good about the efficiency of central office meetings, they resolved to give the checklist a try themselves. Doing so was right in line with Superintendent Nancy Cook's pledge to bring a consistent approach to all levels of the system and to not ask teachers to do anything she and the leadership team weren't willing to try themselves.

Deputy Superintendent Duane Hill was in charge of sending around the agenda for the weekly Monday morning leadership team meetings. The meetings typically went off like clockwork: First, Nancy welcomed the group and gave a big-picture overview of the district's progress toward strategic goals. Then each of the eleven other members of the team took the floor for exactly 10 minutes to report out on the status of their department's work. Lots of information got shared, but no one enjoyed the time. By about halfway through, Duane was not alone in stealing glances at the clock and wishing he could get on with the real work of the week.

Putting the agenda together had always been painless for Duane: he just had his assistant change the dates on the previous agenda and e-mail it to the group on Thursday afternoons (see Exhibit 3.5).

Exhibit 3.5

DRAFT Agenda		
Jackson County Central Office Leadership Team Meeting		
Jackson County Public Schools Leadership Team Meeting Agenda Monday, October 11, 8:00–10:00 a.m.		
Facilitator: Nancy Cook Time keeper: Kim Boylan Note taker: Rodney Solano		
Please submit any presentation slides you will be using at the meeting to Kim Boylan by Friday, October 8		
8:00–8:20	Superintendent's Update	Nancy Cook
8:20–8:30	Curriculum	Kai Peters
8:30–8:40	Technology	Lisa Levy
8:40–8:50	Special Education	Evangeline Zhang
8:50–9:00	Assessment	Brendan Powers
9:00–9:10	Professional Development	Shayna Oh
9:10–9:20	Human Resources	Timothy James
9:20–9:30	Finance & Business Operations	Sammy Taylor
9:30–9:40	Facilities	Eddie Rondo
9:40–9:50	Equity Initiative	Chrystal Samson
9:50–10:00	Looking Ahead	Duane Hill

As Duane reviewed the agenda against the abbreviated version of the Meeting Wise Checklist, he was pleased to see that right off the bat he could check "yes" on more than half of the questions (see Exhibit 3.6). But as he looked at the "nos," he realized that he and Nancy would have plenty to discuss in their standing meeting.

Purpose

Before talking with Nancy, Duane, who was responsible for creating the agenda, spent some time thinking about the purpose of the weekly leadership team meetings. Was it to make district policy? Not really. It was common knowledge that nothing got decided at the Monday meetings. The superintendent was very careful: she ensured that controversial topics occurred off-line so that differences of opinion could be resolved privately without unnecessarily ruffling any feathers.

Was the purpose to make sure the different departments talked to one another, so that they were not stuck in the silos characteristic of so many other districts? Well, if Duane were to be honest, the meetings

Exhibit 3.6

Checklist for DRAFT Agenda Jackson County Central Office Leadership Team Meeting			
		YES	NO
PURPOSE	1. Objectives	☐	☑
	2. Connection	☑	☐
PROCESS	3. Feedback	☐	☑
	4. Activities	☐	☑
	5. Roles	☑	☐
	6. Next steps	☑	☐
	7. Assessment	☐	☑
PREPARATION	8. Materials	☑	☐
	9. Pre-work	☑	☐
PACING	10. Time allocations	☑	☐
	11. Primary objective	☐	☑
	12. Is it realistic?	☑	☐

didn't provide much opportunity for talking *with* anyone. It was more like talking *at* people. And it wasn't particularly clear to the speaker or listeners what anyone was supposed to do with the information that was presented.

Was the purpose to make sure everybody started work at 8:00 a.m. on Monday mornings? If so, there must be a better way to kick off the week! Couldn't they channel the energy of their very talented and committed team—instead of lulling folks into a placid boredom that even free high-end coffee couldn't overcome?

Duane knew that team members used the Monday morning meeting as a chance to put on a show that would make it look like everything was under control in the various departments. But the truth was that, without exception, the people in the room spent much of their week dealing with acute crises or complex, long-term issues. When he sat down with Nancy, he asked her what she thought of using the two hours for collaborative problem solving. To his surprise, she jumped at the suggestion.

Process

Nancy agreed with Duane's argument that if they were to recast Monday morning as a time when individuals could bring a dilemma to the group and get ideas for solving it, they would need to establish clear "norms" of behavior that made people feel safe enough to expose themselves to the group.

They agreed to set aside 20 minutes of the next meeting to engage the group in a conversation around the type of norms that would make it possible for them to give—and receive—feedback on how to deal with complicated problems (see chapter 4 and "Selected Protocols" for guidelines on setting norms).

Nancy also felt that they would need to put quite a bit of structure around the conversation. One of the real benefits of their old way of running meetings was that the strict time limits kept Chief Academic Officer Kai Peters, who seemed to have something to say no matter what the topic, from taking over each meeting. Nancy suggested that, instead of having people hear feedback on how to address their dilemma from the whole group right away, they could start by allowing people five minutes to discuss their ideas in pairs. The next five minutes could then be used to go around the table sharing highlights of these conversations.

Duane appreciated what Nancy was getting at, but felt that they wouldn't be able to do any of the problems justice in five to ten minutes. In the end, Nancy and Duane decided to go for depth over breadth: each Monday, they would make time for two participants to be the subject of a 30-minute Consultancy Protocol.[2] The protocol would allow the presenter to listen silently as others explored the problem and then join in later to work toward a solution. Once the team got the hang of this new format, they could also build in time to talk about how the insights generated to support a particular colleague might apply more broadly.

To model what it would look like to open up one's practice, Nancy agreed to have one of the first consultancies be about her own challenges around providing critical feedback to principals. Technology guru Lisa Levy agreed to bring the second consultancy; she had already told Duane that she needed support in thinking through how to make the transition to the new technology platform as seamless as possible across the district.

Preparation

Leadership team members had been accustomed to setting aside time on Friday to get their presentation slides for Monday in order. Nancy and Duane agreed that the consultancies would be most effective if participants repurposed that time to read through materials provided by the two people presenting dilemmas. They decided to keep their current practice of sending the agenda out on Thursday afternoons.

Pacing

As Duane put times to the activities, he noticed that they had plenty of time to spare. In fact, if they could cut the Norm-Setting Protocol back by five minutes, they could add a third consultancy to the day and get even more deep work done than they had originally hoped.

But was barreling through the agenda the right course? And would it help them achieve their ultimate purpose of encouraging collaborative problem solving? Nancy wondered aloud whether they could just give themselves a little breathing room for a change. What if they built in a 10-minute break, acknowledging for once that drinking coffee and then sitting for two hours was, at the very least, uncomfortable? Also, it wouldn't hurt to give people a little unstructured time to check in with one another either professionally or personally. They felt more like a *group* than a real *team*; maybe having time to just talk would help with that.

That would still leave a full 15 minutes to engage the group in a conversation about how the Consultancy Protocol went and what they might do to adjust the protocol to work even better. They might not need that much time in future meetings; but for the first one, Duane felt strongly that it would help build trust among the team members if they made time for an honest, open conversation about the new approach. That would probably be a lot more constructive than their usual practice of leaving the post-game analysis to water-cooler chatter. Exhibit 3.7 shows the agenda they finally created.

Exhibit 3.7

REVISED Agenda Jackson County Central Office Leadership Team Meeting		
Jackson County Public Schools Leadership Team Meeting Agenda Monday, October 11, 8:00–10:00 a.m.		
Facilitator: Nancy Cook Time keeper: Kim Boylan Note taker: Rodney Solano		
Preparation (approximately an hour): Please read the attached background materials from Nancy and Lisa and come prepared to discuss the dilemmas they have framed.		
8:00–8:10	Welcome	Nancy Cook
8:10–8:30	Norm–Setting Protocol	Duane Hill
8:30–9:00	CONSULTANCY PROTOCOL: How to make difficult conversations with principals more productive	Nancy Cook
9:00–9:10	BREAK	
9:10–9:40	CONSULTANCY PROTOCOL: How to ensure a smooth transition to the new tech platform	Lisa Levy
9:40–9:55	DEBRIEF the Consultancy Protocol 2 min.: silent reflection 3 min.: discussion in pairs 10 min.: group discussion on how to adjust the protocol next time	Duane Hill
9:55–10:00	VOLUNTEERS for next week?	Nancy Cook

At first glance, it may appear that this agenda is not as "meaty" as the typical Jackson County Public Schools leadership team agendas had been. But the team is conducting an important experiment: they are exploring whether it is possible that *less is more* and whether participants might be more engaged if they were actively solving problems and supporting one another rather than reporting out. In our experience, doing a few things deeply can be much more powerful than skimming the surface of a host of issues. And we've never once decided to add some extra breathing space into a meeting and then lived to regret it. For any meeting over 90 minutes, a stretch break can make the whole experience more pleasant—and productive.

✳ ✳ ✳

This example illustrates how putting people in the same room together for a few hours every week by no means guarantees that the group will become cohesive. Leaders need to be intentional in the support they provide around collaboration. Similar intentionality is required when supporting educators in learning how to change their practice, as the next example will show.

TARGETING ADULT LEARNING: SHELDON ACADEMY FACULTY RETREAT

As much as **Principal Maria Diaz** treasured her vacation in July, she couldn't help but relish the promise of a new year that she felt each August. Just before the previous year had ended, Maria and visual art teacher Ari Samson had heard a very inspirational speaker at a conference they attended together. The speaker had reaffirmed Maria's commitment to do more to draw out the creative talents of Sheldon Academy's 750 middle school students.

August 18 was one of only two all-day professional development days in the school calendar. Maria resolved to make the day a truly powerful learning experience for her 40 staff members, as well as an opportunity to encourage a greater emphasis on creativity in the classroom. She drew up a tentative schedule (Exhibit 3.8) for the day and sent it to both Ari and special education teacher Karen McDonald. Maria included some notes on the schedule so that Ari and Karen would understand what she had in mind for the day, and asked for their candid feedback.

Exhibit 3.8

DRAFT Agenda Sheldon Academy Faculty Retreat	
8:00–8:45	WELCOME CIRCLE (Maria) I'll explain that the objective for the day is to understand the importance of creativity and to get energized to give students lots of opportunity to build their creative muscles. (And don't worry . . . I won't forget to describe how they can return to this theme in team meetings throughout the year.) Then we can use a protocol that allows staff members to offer a personal experience in which creativity played an important role in their lives. (I'm thinking this will start our year on a positive note, and it would be good to hear from everyone, especially our 6 new staff members, early in the day.)
8:45–10:15	"CREATIVITY JAM" PRESENTATION (Roy Kim) Roy (the speaker Ari and I heard in June) is amazing. He's got a really inspirational style and has lots of info on the impact high-stakes tests are having on kids, especially middle schoolers. (And he's available on Aug. 18!) We can suggest people read his article in advance.
10:15–10:30	BREAK
10:30–11:45	HIGHLIGHTS FROM ARTS CONFERENCE (Maria & Ari) This is where I'm thinking Ari and I could share some of our biggest takeaways from the conference.
11:45–12:45	LUNCH We have the budget to provide this. Last year, we did Indian food. Any ideas for something fun?
12:45–1:45	DEPARTMENTAL DISCUSSIONS ON CREATIVITY (Breakout sessions) Here we could give departmental teams a chance to process what they learned in the morning and come up with ideas for how to apply their learning to teaching in their subject areas.
1:45–2:45	OUR CREATIVE VISION (Roy Kim) I can see if Roy could stay through lunch, sit in on some of the departmental discussions, and then lead the whole group in sharing the ideas that came up in the breakout sessions. Maybe ask him to facilitate a discussion around revising our mission statement to capture our collective beliefs about the importance of creativity?
2:45–3:00	CLOSING (Karen, would you be game to lead this?) We can have folks do a quick survey on how the day went and then end with sharing their biggest hope for the coming year. We can capture those hopes and display them on the bulletin board outside the main office for all the kids to see on their first day back.

When Karen and Ari looked at the schedule, they smiled. Maria had made a big effort last year to transform faculty meetings into opportunities for professional growth and community building. She'd really overhauled her approach to meetings, as could be seen by the fact that they could now check "yes" on 10 of the 12 checklist questions. But the two "no" responses (questions 4 and 11) were by no means trivial. They felt strongly that the *activities* Maria proposed were not actually in service of what they knew to be her *primary objective*: increasing the emphasis on creativity in Sheldon classrooms. The problem, they explained when they talked with her, was that the plan Maria laid out required adults to sit through hours of hearing about what other people thought about creativity, but didn't provide any space for teachers to do hands-on work that could spark real changes in their practice.

Ari had also enjoyed the speaker from the conference; in an ideal world, it would be nice to have faculty hear from Professor Kim. But they had only seven hours to play with, and it just didn't make sense to put nearly half that time in the hands of an outside speaker. So Ari and Karen proposed making a major change in the *type* of activities teachers would be asked to do throughout the day. They felt sure that reading the article ahead of time and hearing 15 minutes' worth of highlights from Maria and Ari's experience would provide all the background teachers needed. If the goal was to change practice, then they needed to give teachers most of the day to work in small groups designing specific strategies for infusing a more creative element into their existing lesson plans.

Ari and Karen were heartened when, two days after their conversation, they received the following revision from Maria (Exhibit 3.9).

In this case, checklist question 4 ("Have we chosen challenging activities that advance the meeting objectives and engage all participants?") helped Ari and Karen provide very specific feedback to their principal about how the professional development experience could be improved. Maria was open to the feedback, so the revised plan for the staff retreat at Sheldon Academy involves a whole lot less sitting and listening and a whole lot more working and moving than the original one.

Maria's plan to use a few strategically chosen protocols increases the chances that everyone will stay fully engaged throughout the seven-hour period. The Maître d'Protocol, which involves having the facilitator ask people to quickly group and regroup in standing "tables

Exhibit 3.9

REVISED Agenda Sheldon Academy Faculty Retreat	
8:00–8:45	WELCOME CIRCLE (led by Maria) • Meeting objective: build more creativity into lesson plans across the school • Example of personal experience with creativity from Maria • Maître d'Protocol: exploring personal experience with creativity
8:45–9:00	ARTS CONFERENCE HIGHLIGHTS (led by Maria & Ari)
9:00–10:15	CREATIVITY DISCUSSION (led by department chairs) • In departmental teams, brainstorm ideas for how to incorporate creativity into lesson plans and assignments for the first unit of the year
10:15–10:30	BREAK
10:30–11:45	CREATIVITY DISCUSSION (led by grade-level team leaders) • In grade-level teams, share brainstormed ideas and discuss how to integrate them across subject areas
11:45–1:00	LUNCH–MAKE YOUR OWN PIZZA (Everyone) • With a prize for the group that makes the most creative one!
1:00–2:25	COLLABORATIVE LESSON PLANNING (Everyone) • Teachers work in pairs to revise a lesson plan for use in the first weeks of school
2:25–2:45	GALLERY WALK (Everyone) • One member of each pair stays at table to share the lesson plan with others who come by • Switch halfway through so that each person gets to do a gallery walk
2:45–3:00	CLOSING (led by Karen) • Quick survey on how the day went • Share biggest hope for the coming year (for later post on bulletin board at main entrance)

for 2" (or 3, or 4) and then respond to discussion prompts, would get the day started on an active note and allow everyone to tap into their own creative experience.[3] The gallery walk would give people a chance to both showcase their products and see what their colleagues have created, getting the group moving again just when their energy might be flagging, and helping increase the chances that good ideas hatched between teacher pairs could be shared more broadly.

✻ ✻ ✻

Sheldon's example shows how thinking through the purpose, process, preparation, and pacing of a meeting can set up a large group to have a powerful collective experience over the course of a daylong retreat. But even short, one-on-one meetings can benefit from attention to these things, as seen in the next example. The following example is written from the perspective of a parent, an important educator in the life of a child, but could just as easily be from the perspective of a teacher—or from anyone who wants something specific out of a meeting with another person and wants to make the meeting more purposeful and successful.

TARGETING OUTCOMES: HIGH SCHOOL PARENT/TEACHER CONFERENCE

Mitchell Nelson knew that communication with teachers could be a key to his daughter's academic success. He had never missed a single back-to-school night or parent/teacher conference. Yet he always came away from the conferences vaguely dissatisfied. The time was always so short, with a few minutes for pleasantries and then a bunch of general statements from the teacher. He never felt like he learned anything specific that could help him support his daughter. But here it was, second semester, and her latest report card clearly showed she was in trouble. He wanted to reach out for an extra conversation with the teacher, and this time he didn't want to come away feeling empty-handed. Before pressing "send" on the following e-mail (see Exhibit 3.10), he paused.

Exhibit 3.10

DRAFT Request
Parent/Teacher Conference

Dear Ms. Prospect,

I'm concerned about Shari's most recent grade in biology, so I'm writing to see if you might have time next week to meet. Would you be available any morning next week before 9:00 a.m. or Thursday at noon?

Thank you very much,
Mitchell Nelson (Shari's dad)

Mitchell took a look at the Meeting Wise Checklist that a member of the Home and School Association had recently shown him. Would he be better off if he sent the teacher a formal agenda? His first impulse was to laugh . . . he pictured how chagrined his 15-year-old would be if he showed up with a minute-by-minute timetable for the conference. No, following the checklist to the letter would feel uncomfortable, at least for him and maybe for Shari's teacher. But could it help him write an e-mail that would make it more likely that he'd have a good conversation with Ms. Prospect?

Purpose

First of all, Mitchell decided to be more specific about what he wanted. He actually didn't mind so much about Shari's third-quarter grade. The thing that worried him was how helpless she seemed whenever her homework called for learning from the huge textbook that she kept on a shelf in the kitchen. He knew she couldn't be spending much time with that book because it spent an awful lot of time on that shelf. Also, she had stopped asking for his help with biology homework because every time he encouraged her to look up the answer in the book, she rolled her eyes and told him that you weren't really supposed to *read* it. Was that true? Back when he was a kid, by the end of the year, you were supposed to have read the textbook pretty much cover to cover. Had things changed? Or was his daughter avoiding the book because she was unable to make sense of it? Mitchell realized that what he most wanted to know was whether the teacher felt his daughter had the reading skills she needed to learn high school biology. If she didn't, he wanted to know what could be done to catch her up.

Process

For the kind of meeting he was looking for, Mitchell decided that the questions on the process section of the checklist could be safely ignored.

Preparation

He wasn't sure if there was something he could do ahead of time. So he decided to ask the teacher if there were materials he should review. He also wondered whether the teacher might be able to arrange for an assessment of Shari's reading ability before the conference.

Pacing

Meetings on conference days were harried events, with teachers having to cycle parents through 10-minute slots that just never seemed long enough. For this meeting, Mitchell wanted to have a real conversation, and figured they would need at least 20 minutes to do that. So he planned to ask for the time he thought was necessary, and then be sure to keep an eye on the clock during the meeting. His revised e-mail is shown in Exhibit 3.11.

This example shows that not every meeting needs to have a formal agenda. But, any time two or more people set aside time to have a discussion, each participant has at least an implicit agenda. Communicating ahead of time about what that discussion will cover can make a big difference in whether you can achieve your desired outcome. Identifying things to do in advance of the meeting can also make it more likely that you will get to the heart of the matter in limited time.

Exhibit 3.11

REVISED Request
Parent/Teacher Conference

Dear Ms. Prospect,

I'm writing to see if you might have 20–30 minutes sometime next week to discuss Shari's learning. I'm wondering:

- How thoroughly are students required to read the textbook?
- Do you think Shari has a reading problem? If so, would it be possible to check in with a reading specialist?
- What could I be doing at home to help her?
- What could the school do?

Would you be available any morning next week before 9:00 a.m. or Thursday at noon? Please let me know if there anything I could do ahead of time to get ready for our discussion.

Thank you very much,
Mitchell Nelson (Shari's dad)

✳ ✳ ✳

In this example, Mitchell used the checklist quietly on his own to help him think about a meeting he was hoping to have. The following example shows how the checklist can be used similarly when you are asked to attend a meeting and you want to weigh in about how the meeting is designed.

TARGETING PROBLEM SOLVING OVER COMPLIANCE: STATEWIDE QUARTERLY SUPERINTENDENTS' MEETING

■ **Superintendent Jack Carson had become** accustomed to finding the quarterly superintendents' meetings at the office of the state commissioner to be deadly dull. But when he received the draft agenda for the upcoming meeting, his stomach fell. The topic was going to be on helping districts comply with the state's new teacher evaluation system. He couldn't afford to be bored at this one—implementing the new system was by far the most pressing issue in his district, and he needed all the support he could get. Here is the agenda he received (Exhibit 3.12).

The cover letter from Commissioner Paul Randall had said "feedback welcome." Normally, Jack wouldn't have taken the time to give any feedback because he was busy and wasn't entirely sure the commissioner

Exhibit 3.12

DRAFT Agenda Statewide Quarterly Superintendents' Meeting	
Quarterly Superintendents' Meeting	
TOPIC:	Preparing to Implement the Teacher Evaluation System
DATE:	December 5, 8:00–9:30 a.m.
PREPARATION	Read the attached regulations and timelines
8:00–8:30	Review regulations and timelines
8:30–9:15	Panel of superintendents who are piloting the system
9:15–9:30	Questions & comments

actually expected or wanted it. But this time, he really needed some help, so he resolved that he would pick up the phone that afternoon and offer some suggestions. Before he did, he looked at the Meeting Wise Checklist (Exhibit 3.13). There was no way he was going to actually walk the commissioner through the checklist, but Jack thought it might help him figure out what his own priorities were for the conversation and give him some ideas about how to frame his feedback.

Purpose

Jack saw right away that were lots of ways in which the meeting could be improved. But he knew the conversation with the commissioner would be short, so he decided to focus his attention on what mattered to him most: that he be able to leave the meeting with a clear sense of how to address some of the problems with the teacher evaluation system that were most pressing to him.

Exhibit 3.13

Checklist for DRAFT Agenda Quarterly Superintendents' Meeting		YES	NO
PURPOSE	1. Objectives	☑	☐
	2. Connection	☐	☑
PROCESS	3. Feedback	☐	☑
	4. Activities	☐	☑
	5. Roles	☐	☑
	6. Next steps	☐	☑
	7. Assessment	☐	☑
PREPARATION	8. Materials	☑	☐
	9. Pre-work	☑	☐
PACING	10. Time allocations	☑	☐
	11. Primary objective	☑	☐
	12. Is it realistic?	☑	☐

Process, Preparation, and Pacing

One of the things that drove Jack crazy about state state-level meetings was that they lumped all of the superintendents together, even though the districts varied widely in terms of size, students served, the quality of their relationships with unions, and their most pressing instructional issues. The draft agenda allowed a mere 15 minutes for questions; with his luck, someone from one of the suburban districts would raise a point that had little bearing on his situation, and before he knew it, the meeting would be adjourned. What he wanted—and what he believed all of the superintendents could benefit from—was dedicated time to talk with colleagues who shared his circumstances.

Jack decided that he would recommend that the commissioner ask superintendents to e-mail their questions ahead of time. That way, Commissioner Randall would see the great range of issues that people faced. There could be a few minutes at the beginning of the meeting during which the commissioner could address topics that pertained to everyone. Then they could hear from the panel, which sounded useful. But there needed to be a large chunk of breakout time at the end of the meeting when Jack could discuss issues with the five other superintendents of similar districts. If someone from the commissioner's office could sit with them and help them sort things out, maybe they could get somewhere.

Jack made his case to the commissioner, who seemed appreciative of the feedback. In fact, he asked if Jack would be willing to lead the breakout session with his small group. Jack closed his eyes as he replied that he would be happy to. He smiled—both at the thought that he should have seen that coming, and at the fact that next month's meeting was a lot less likely to feel like a waste of his time than it would have if he hadn't spoken up (see Exhibit 3.14).

* * *

The Meeting Wise Checklist can be used subtly, and by participants as well as facilitators. Chapter 6 will address head-on the role of participants in improving meeting quality, but for now let's just say that if you point out problems with a meeting that you have to attend, don't be surprised if you end up becoming part of the solution (and don't let that stop you from making suggestions!).

Exhibit 3.14

REVISED Agenda Statewide Quarterly Superintendents' Meeting	
Quarterly Superintendents' Meeting	
TOPIC:	Preparing to Implement the Teacher Evaluation System
DATE:	December 5, 8:00–9:30 a.m.
PREPARATION: (about an hour)	• Read the attached regulations and timelines • E-mail questions to Sid_Howe@state.edu by 5:00 p.m. on December 1.
SCHEDULE:	
8:00–8:20	Address general questions
8:20–8:50	Panel of superintendents who are piloting the system
8:50–9:30	Breakouts to discuss issues specific to district type • Urban districts: led by Jack Carson • Suburban districts: led by Kate McPhee • Rural districts: led by Mandy Meyers

All of the examples we have discussed so far have focused on groups who that have a clear reason to work together and formal obligation to attend meetings, to "comply" as well as learn together. But there are many groups throughout the education sector that meet regularly but have a much weaker claim on participants' time. To explore how the Meeting Wise Checklist can help under those circumstances, we now turn to our final example.

TARGETING CONNECTIONS: NATIONAL ANTI-BULLYING NETWORK VIRTUAL MEETING

■ **The National Anti-Bullying Network includes** representatives from schools, parent groups, health organizations, and government offices. At last count, 64 people had registered to take part in their monthly hour-long virtual meetings, which could be accessed via phone or videoconference software. But enrollment had dropped in recent months, even though Network leader Carl Chomsky knew that bullying was as big an issue as ever. How could he reinvigorate participation in a group with a noble purpose but voluntary involvement? How could he set things up so that people felt lucky to be part of the calls and felt that their collective investment over the course of the year made a difference? Exhibit 3.15 shows the agenda for the upcoming meeting.

When Carl looked at the draft agenda, he was puzzled about why people wouldn't find the network conference calls irresistible. Every month, he put together a panel of experts who were doing cutting-edge work in a field that members held close to their hearts. Speakers were always extremely prepared, distilling their work into concise remarks that helped renew a sense of both urgency and promise. Why weren't people burning up the phone lines? Carl reviewed his agenda against the Meeting Wise Checklist (Exhibit 3.16) for insights.

As Carl looked at the checklist, and then back at his agenda, he saw that the information in the meetings was only flowing only in one direction: from the speakers out to the dwindling virtual audience. The checklist made him realize that he had never sought direct participant feedback about the meetings, so he created an online survey about the conference calls that was loosely based on checklist questions. The feedback he received gave him lots to think about.

Exhibit 3.15

DRAFT Agenda Anti-Bullying Network Virtual Meeting	
National Anti-Bullying Network December 5, 12:00–1:00 EST Call in Number: 1-800-495-0342; Pin: 170404 Video conference available at www.videomeeting.com	
Purpose: To keep all members informed about the work that is happening in schools, legislative offices, and research institutions so that we can end bullying NOW.	
12:00–12:15	Success Stories from Schools Principal Sandra Shore, Canyon High School
12:15–12:30	Legislative Round-Up Representative Steve Montego, fifth-district
12:30–12:50	Research Update—Role of Bystanders Professor Elizabeth Eden
12:50–1:00	Preview of Next Session's Speakers Network Leader Carl Chomsky

Exhibit 3.16

		YES	NO
Checklist for DRAFT Agenda **Anti-Bullying Network Virtual Meeting**			
PURPOSE	1. Objectives	☑	☐
	2. Connection	☐	☑
PROCESS	3. Feedback	☐	☑
	4. Activities	☐	☑
	5. Roles	☐	☑
	6. Next steps	☐	☑
	7. Assessment	☐	☑
PREPARATION	8. Materials	☐	☑
	9. Pre-work	☐	☑
PACING	10. Time allocations	☑	☐
	11. Primary objective	☐	☑
	12. Is it realistic?	☑	☐

Purpose

Carl was glad to hear that members were excited about the purpose. However, they did not see a sense of connection between one *meeting* and the next, so they felt that it didn't matter much whether they missed a particular session. They also didn't see much connection between one *speaker* and the next, so they felt free to join the call late or leave it early. Carl revised his plan to focus on a particular theme across speakers (which would also probably mean finding a new speaker, since the ones he had lined up were planning to talk about different things). He wanted to think more about how this theme might connect to the next meeting.

Process, Preparation, and Pacing

Although members reported that they believed the speakers were excellent, they noted that network was not taking advantage of technology that would allow for richer engagement of participants. True, the network provided the option that members could participate via video conferencing software. But folks who logged in were disappointed to find that they got little more than a talking head. Carl resolved to work with speakers to develop visual materials to go along with their comments, and to work with his tech support staff to use the videoconferencing platform to create a sense of virtual community.

Carl learned that while he personally found the speakers to be concise, most of the members who responded to his survey felt that the individual speakers all went on too long. So Carl decided to shorten their presentations, freeing up 15 minutes for virtual breakouts so that members could engage with one another around the meeting's theme.

He also decided to use the last few minutes of each session to get in-the-moment feedback from participants about what worked and what didn't. He knew he couldn't keep sending out online surveys, but he wanted to get a read on how his adjustments were being received. With all this in mind, he revised his agenda (see Exhibit 3.17).

Exhibit 3.17

REVISED Agenda
Anti-Bullying Network Virtual Meeting

National Anti-Bullying Network
December 5, 12:00–1:00 EST
Call in Number: 1-800-495-0342; Pin: 170404
Video conference available at www.videomeeting.com

NETWORK PURPOSE: To keep all members informed about the work that is happening in schools, legislative offices, and research institutions so that we can end bullying NOW.

TODAY'S THEME: Role of guidance counselors

12:00–12:10	Success Stories from Schools • Principal Sandra Shore, Canyon High School
12:10–12:20	Legislative Round-Up • Representative Steve Montego, fifth-district
12:20–12:30	Research Update—Counseling for Counselors • Professor Ziv Miller
12:30–12:50	What does this mean for the field? What are the challenges schools and districts are facing? • Virtual breakout discussions
12:50–1:00	Preview of January theme: Supporting Families; Feedback on this session • Network Leader Carl Chomsky

This example illustrates the power of asking meeting participants for ideas about how to make a meeting more effective. It also points out that, even—or perhaps especially—for virtual meetings, participants are often eager to connect with one another and the topic in a meaningful way. The advantage a meeting has over a newsletter, after all, is that it happens in real time with real people. When planning a meeting, it is important to keep this idea front and center, and to be sure that you make the most of your context to allow for people to really collaborate on ideas, to problem-solve, and to learn from one another.

* * *

All of the examples illustrate the value of getting multiple perspectives when planning an agenda. Never plan alone. If the meeting is important enough to put on people's calendars, it is important either formally or informally discuss the agenda with others. We are continually amazed to see how even a 10-minute consultation with a colleague—either one who will be attending the meeting or one who is blissfully ignorant of the meeting dynamics and can offer an objective view—always offers something helpful to think about.

THE MEETING WISE AGENDA TEMPLATE

This chapter describes what it looks like when thoughtful educators use the Meeting Wise Checklist to reflect on an existing agenda draft and think about improvements. But what if you *began* the agenda-making process with the checklist in mind? Wouldn't that be even more efficient? For recurring meetings, the agenda will probably look pretty similar from one meeting to the next. Coming up with a standard agenda template helps with consistency and frees up time so you can spend more time thinking about the content of the agenda and less time worrying about how to format your document.

With this in mind, we worked with educators to develop the Meeting Wise Agenda Template (Exhibit 3.18). An electronic version of the template is freely available at http://www.gse.harvard.edu/meetingwise.

Exhibit 3.18

Meeting Wise Agenda Template

MEETING AGENDA
[date], [start time] – [end time]
[location]

TOPIC:	Attendees: **5** Facilitator: Note taker: Timekeeper:

MEETING OBJECTIVES: ❶
- [objective 1]
- [objective 2]
- [objective 3]

TO PREPARE FOR THIS MEETING, PLEASE:
- Read this agenda [optional: and reply to (name) with feedback by (date)] **8** **9**
- [other pre-work task]

Schedule [XX minutes] **12**

TIME **10**	MINUTES	ACTIVITY **4**
X:XX-X:XX	X	Check-in and review how objectives of this meeting connect to our ongoing work **2**
X:XX-X:XX	X	Review next steps from our previous meeting
X:XX-X:XX	X	Review plus/deltas from our previous meeting **3** | Plus	Delta
---	---
• [pluses from previous meeting]	• [deltas from previous meeting]	
X:XX-X:XX	X	[objective 1] **11**
X:XX-X:XX	X	[objective 2]
X:XX-X:XX	X	[objective 3]
X:XX-X:XX	X	Review next steps from this meeting **6**
X:XX-X:XX	X	Assess what worked well about this meeting and what we would have liked to change **7** | Plus	Delta
---	---
•	•	

KEY

1. Objectives	**4.** Activities	**7.** Assessments	**10.** Time allocations
2. Connection	**5.** Roles	**8.** Materials	**11.** Primary objectives
3. Feedback	**6.** Next steps	**9.** Pre-work	**12.** Realistic

If you use this template *as is* to create an agenda, you will see how it nudges you toward answering "yes" on nearly all of the twelve questions on the Meeting Wise Checklist. But you are, of course, welcome to *customize* the template so that it fits well with the needs of a particular set of meetings.

Try It Yourself
Use the Checklist to Design an Agenda

1. Think about a meeting you will be having in the near future, ideally one that is in a series of recurring meetings, some of which have already happened.

2. Look at the agendas from the previous meetings in the series, evaluating at least one of them against the Meeting Wise Checklist.

3. Think about how you might rework a past agenda to make it more meeting wise, then create an agenda for your upcoming meeting that takes your ideas into account. Feel free to use the Meeting Wise Agenda Template if you think it would be helpful.

4. Share the agenda with your meeting buddy and ask for feedback.

SECTION II WORKING DIFFERENTLY

4

SETTING UP FOR SUCCESS

CREATING AN EFFECTIVE AGENDA is an important first step toward having a great meeting. There are also several other things you need to do between crafting the agenda and enacting it to set the meeting up for success. In this chapter, we'll start by discussing the foundational tasks, then we'll describe the recurring tasks that are good to take care of before each individual meeting.

FOUNDATIONAL SETUP TASKS

With a series of meetings, the key is to avoid reinventing the wheel for each meeting. Instead, figure out what you can make consistent across meetings, and then invest in creating structures and routines that establish a basis for how the group operates. Foundational tasks include setting group norms, acknowledging work style preferences, developing an agenda template, and making a documentation plan. Ideally, you would do these things when you launch a team or at the beginning of a series of meetings, but it's also okay to do them midstream if they are not yet in place.

Setting Group Norms

Norms are ground rules for how members of a group agree to behave during a meeting. There are lots of ways to approach setting norms (see the Norm-Setting Protocol in Selected Protocols for an example). Some approaches start with a blank slate and allow norms to evolve from the group. Others involve proposing a set of norms and then allowing a group to discuss and refine them. When we take the route of starting with a proposed list of norms, we typically include:

1. **Assume positive intentions.** Take the premise that everyone in the group is acting out of a desire to work toward our shared goal of helping all students learn. When followed, this norm is experienced as a silent reminder to oneself: *this person wants to do well by children, too.*

2. **Take an inquiry stance.** Ask questions that allow insight into a colleague's point of view. To put this norm into practice, we often recommend that team members use sentence starters such as, "What led you to conclude . . . ?" "I'm hearing you say . . . is that correct?" and the simple but often effective, "I'm wondering what you mean by . . . ?" At first, these words can feel forced. But in time they can become such a natural part of the way the group communicates that people hardly realize they are using them.

3. **Ground statements in evidence.** Make a conscious effort to cite data or offer a rationale when explaining one's point of view. Sentence starters such as, "I see . . . ," "I noticed that . . . ," and "I saw evidence of . . . " can make it more likely that statements are not laced with adjectives and proclamations. We often point out that this norm can be hard to follow, and encourage participants to support one another in using it by feeling free to ask, "What's your evidence?"

4. **Stick to protocol.** Stay within the guidelines of any discussion protocol used during a meeting, even if it feels constraining (see chapter 2 for a discussion of what protocols are and why it is important to stick to them).

5. **Start and end on time.** Enough said. In our experience, this one is enormously important for developing the trust and respect of all meeting participants.

6. **Be here now.** Stay on task. No surfing the web or texting during meetings. You may be surprised at how relieved your group is when this norm is consistently honored and enforced.

Whether you start with a proposed list or have the group generate norms from scratch, set aside time to come to a shared understanding of what each norm means and what it would look like if it were followed—or not. Then discuss what you will do when norms are violated.

We've seen groups come up with all kinds of strategies: hold up yellow or red paper to signal a violation, put $1 in a violations jar that goes toward a charity or a treat for the group, sing a song (the violator has a solo). Some groups go for fun and silly to take some of the stigma out of both calling and being called on norms violations. Some groups go more low-key. Either way, the group's commitment to some way of acknowledging breaches of norms will authorize the facilitator—and indeed, all participants—to follow through.

The "right" list of norms will vary from group to group. Some other common and helpful norms we have seen are "Watch your airtime" and "What happens in this room stays in this room." One thing to keep in mind is that having a shorter list may make it more likely that everyone will remember what's on it. Prioritize what feels most important, or collapse a couple of related ideas into a single norm. Once you've agreed on a list, decide how you'll keep the norms top of mind for everyone. We've seen teams do this by posting norms on the wall, creating norms tents for each table, or even typing norms into the header or footer of the agenda template.

The most important thing about norms is being sure to return to them regularly. If all you do is go through the motions of setting norms but don't refer to them again, you have wasted your time. But if you lean on them when the going gets tough and modify them as needed, norms will provide a solid foundation for your collaborative work.

Acknowledging Work Style Preferences

When collaborating, it is helpful for members of a group to have an opportunity to know and understand one another's preferred ways of working. Who in the room needs the big picture first, and who wants the details? Who's inclined to charge ahead and take action, and who is more inclined to take the time to elicit multiple perspectives?

There are multiple tools for understanding and naming preferences, ranging from formal personality-trait assessments to more informal ones, like the Compass Points Protocol.[1]

Liz's most poignant experience with the power of knowing and naming preferences came when she was a principal in North Carolina. She and the teachers had just done an activity in which they stacked four color cards, each of which had a set of adjectives and descriptions of preferences for working in groups (a variation of a protocol called True Colors™).[2] As they looked around the table to see what color everyone had on top, one colleague said to another, "Oh, you're a *yellow*—that's why you've been driving me crazy the last two years! You like details and I like to charge ahead. It's actually good you're a yellow because otherwise things would be really sloppy around here, including our testing program, which I'm so glad you're in charge of. I bet I've been driving you crazy, too. Now I get it." Thus was launched a conversation full of laughter and "a-ha" moments. At last, the faculty had a way to talk about the different ways they approached collaborative work. Throughout the year, they could then say things like, "I know I'm being blue here, but it would really help me if we could . . ." and "You're being so red right now. Let's slow down for a minute" or "We all need to go green for a few minutes and think about what we're trying to accomplish."

Really productive teams and meetings make good use of people's preferences and give space and modes for multiple ways of thinking and doing.

Developing Agenda Templates

As we mentioned at the end of chapter 3, it is efficient to determine the basic format of the agenda and then stick to it for a series of meetings. If this template is also used by other teams in the organization, that consistency helps build in efficiency and consistency across the organization—provided, of course, that the template serves each group's purpose well. In our own work, we use the Meeting Wise Agenda Template for all our core team meetings. These sessions demand a formal approach that allows a group of four to eight people (sometimes across multiple locations) to collaborate for a period of months or years. For one-on-one meetings, we use a much simpler template that dispenses with the official-looking table format and focuses on naming our objectives and allotting times to addressing each one. For professional development meetings, our agenda template is basically a lesson plan.

Regardless of the approach you take, be sure not to etch your meeting agenda templates in stone. As you respond to feedback about how meetings are going, you may end up needing to adjust the templates themselves so you can best serve the evolving needs of the group.

Keeping Track of Your Work

Effective meetings are going to generate lots of stuff—not just agendas and notes but work products as well. An important foundational setup task, then, is to decide where all meeting documents will live and how each meeting will be documented. Store meeting materials electronically so that meeting members don't need to rely on their own filing system to find what they need. If the information in documents is confidential, your best bet is a password-protected part of your organization's website or a secured shared drive. For groups working with less sensitive information, there are a number of online storage platforms that are quite convenient and either free or low-cost.

Then establish a consistent approach for documenting what happens in a meeting. After experimenting with several strategies, we've settled on the practice of having the note taker type directly into the meeting agenda document as the meeting unfolds. Taking notes in real time means that the note taker's job is finished the moment the meeting is adjourned, with no need for "Type up the minutes" to end up on anyone's to-do list.

We put notes in blue font; this makes it easy to distinguish between what was present in the original agenda and what was added during the meeting. Discussion and decisions associated with a particular agenda item are entered below that item, and there are dedicated "next steps" places right on the agenda for capturing what has been done so far and what everyone is promising to do in the future.

As you create your documentation system, consider making agendas *live shared documents*, and let participants know they need to bring a laptop or tablet to each meeting. With this approach, people can log on to the agenda to see the record of the meeting as the note taker captures it. This can be particularly helpful when participants are calling in from multiple locations, since it provides a sense of immediacy that can be lost on a typical conference call. When you have a shared document, it also opens up the possibility of deputizing a backup note taker. That way, whenever the note taker is speaking or gets distracted, there is a record—and the note taker is less likely to feel sidelined or overwhelmed by the job.

Arrange your system so that it is easy for participants to find information when they need it. Our biggest innovation in this regard is what we have come to call the "rolling agenda"—we allow one long, electronic document to evolve over the course of a series of meetings, making sure the most recent agenda is always at the top. Eventually, the rolling agenda contains the agendas for every meeting in a series, in reverse order, so that the information from all our meetings is captured in one easily searchable place.

Finally, consider creating a meeting summary either at the top of your rolling agenda or as a separate document linked to individual agendas (see Exhibit 4.1). The meeting summary captures key information like meeting objectives, decisions, and next steps for a series of meetings. This can be a helpful place to keep track of what you've done so far and also of what you hope to do in your upcoming meetings.

RECURRING SETUP TASKS

In addition to the foundational setup tasks for the series, there are also a number of recurring tasks to do before each meeting. These include sending the agenda out ahead of time, arranging logistics, and getting your head ready. Each of these may seem like little things, but doing

Exhibit 4.1

Sample Meeting Summary Template			
	MEETING 1	MEETING 2	MEETING 3	MEETING 4
MEETING OBJECTIVES				
DECISIONS				
NEXT STEPS				

them all well can make the difference between a meeting that soars and one that falls flat.

Send Agenda to Participants

You spent time putting together a thoughtful agenda that you believe will advance an important purpose. So be sure to get that good thinking into participants' hands ahead of time!

How far in advance should the agenda go out? For most meetings, a week is ideal. That's respectful of participants' professional and personal lives (which most likely don't revolve around preparing for the meeting that you worked so hard to design). If you are asking people to read something substantial, produce a document, or think deeply about an issue, you may need to give them more time than that.

Sometimes, though, it's not realistic to give people a week's notice. We find that sending out an agenda within 24 hours of a meeting is usually better than not sending it out at all. If that's the case, we realize we can't expect people to do much preparation other than read the agenda, but at least we know they are walking into the meeting aware of the purpose and the plan, which is a good place to start. If the meeting requires serious preparation to make it worthwhile and you just can't get the agenda and preparation assignment out far enough in advance, try to reschedule. Better to postpone than to forge ahead with a meeting that doesn't use people's time well.

When to send out the agenda also depends on whether it invites feedback. We find that when we do ask, we often get excellent suggestions for shifting our purpose or activities or making sure that our plan is realistic. Also, we've seen that inviting feedback has this side benefit: even if participants do not suggest revisions, they often feel better about going with an agenda they at least had the *option* to weigh in on. But keep in mind that if you are not willing to adjust the agenda (or if you suspect that opening things up will bring in competing counteragendas), there is no point in requesting feedback and letting people think they have more influence than they actually do.

Arrange Logistics

There are a lot of things that won't be in your control once real people walk in the door and the meeting gets under way; however, paying attention to some comparatively easy but important logistics can head off some problems. We recommend thinking through the following issues well ahead of time.

1. **Space.** Make sure that you have booked a room that is the right size and shape for the activities you plan on doing. Decide how you want to arrange the furniture so that it will support the kind of interpersonal dynamic you are shooting for. If possible, set things up so that people can all see one another.

2. **Supplies.** Acquire the chart paper, markers, sticky notes, dry-erase markers, handouts, and any other materials that you might need. (We know some groups that include chocolate on their required list for every meeting!) Some groups bring a small plastic container with an array of standard supplies to every meeting; others bring just what they need for a particular meeting.

3. **Name cards.** Prepare name cards if needed—and if anyone doesn't know the others' names, *they're needed*. We like to use name tents made of card stock or 5" × 7" index cards folded in half lengthwise. They are easier to see than wearable tags (although such tags can also be helpful if people are going to be moving and mingling). Another advantage to using name tents is that you can preassign seating, which is particularly helpful if you want participants get to know new people, or if you think some people may be less distracted if their seats are chosen for them.

4. **Refreshments.** Think about what sustenance is required, given the time of day and who can bring it. In the first draft of this book, we neglected to say that having food and drink at a meeting can have a huge impact on how happy and productive participants are (even though we both firmly believe this is true). We heard back loud and clear from the educators who reviewed our manuscript that we needed to point out the importance of food and drink, especially at long meetings. A little refreshment can go a long way to helping people sustain their attention and feel welcome in a meeting.

5. **Technology.** Decide what technology you will need and make sure that you know whom to call for technical assistance if something goes wrong. We highly recommend testing technology enough in advance of the meeting so that there's time for troubleshooting. At least for us, there seems to be a consistent inverse truth—the less time we allow for technology troubleshooting, the more likely there is to be a problem.

Get Your Head Ready

The final setup task to do before each meeting is getting your proverbial "head in the game." Although you have done a lot of thinking to produce the agenda, you may need to write some additional notes to help you remember your plan and to parse out the time in a more fine-grained way than you did in the public version of the agenda. Sometime this requires nothing more than jotting time allocations and things to remember right onto the agenda. But other times you may want to do a full-blown facilitator's agenda, complete with protocol instructions and notes about technology and materials.[3]

There is also a mental aspect to getting ready for a meeting that goes beyond anything you write down. Taking a few minutes to visualize a successful meeting and anticipate challenges, much as an athlete or a performer might do, will help you be truly prepared. Questions to ponder include:

- What do I already know about the culture and habits of the group and of individuals?

- What do I already know about myself vis-à-vis this meeting? Do I feel really strongly about something that might interfere with my ability to facilitate? Do I have particular relationships with participants that are assets or liabilities as I facilitate?

- What's going to be hard about this meeting? Where is it potentially going to go off the rails?

- What will this meeting look and sound like if it's a great success?

It can also be helpful to get clear about what kind of meeting you are about to have.

- Is it a decision-making meeting? Then be sure to make decisions!

- Is it a design meeting? Then foster a generative spirit, not a critical one.

- Is it a problem-solving meeting? Then be sure to both diagnose the problem and generate ideas for solutions.

- Is it a brainstorming meeting? Then don't let people narrow too soon, and work on making sure all voices and ideas are heard.

- Is it a trust-building meeting? Then tune in to how people are interacting.

Having the kind of meeting broadly in mind can help you be prepared to handle whatever may come up during the meeting. For easy reference, Exhibit 4.2 lists the things you can do before a meeting even starts to help set yourself up for success.

Exhibit 4.2

Foundational and Recurring Meeting Setup Tasks	
FOUNDATIONAL SETUP TASKS	**RECURRING SETUP TASKS**

• Set group norms
• Acknowledge work style preferences
• Develop agenda template
• Make documentation plan
	• Send agenda to participants
	• Arrange logistics
	  • Space
	  • Supplies
	  • Name cards
	  • Refreshments
	  • Technology
	• Get your head ready

Try It Yourself
Set Yourself Up for Success

1. To set yourself up for facilitating the meeting you planned at the end of chapter 3, look at the foundational setup tasks and *pick one* to tackle before you facilitate that meeting, if they're not already in place. If you need a thought partner, check in with your meeting buddy.

2. Look at the list of recurring tasks and circle those where you have the most room for improvement, and then pay particular attention to doing these tasks before your next meeting.

Note: Read chapter 5 before actually facilitating the meeting.

5

WISE FACILITATION

Y OUR GROUP HAS NOW made long-term investments that will help it
function effectively. As facilitator, you have gotten all of your mental and logistical ducks in a row. The agenda is set, and it's time to actually have the meeting. The challenge is that no matter how carefully
you've crafted the agenda, no matter whether you've checked "yes" for
every item in the checklist and carefully prepared all the details, once
you enter the meeting room, things rarely go as exactly as planned.
That's because when human beings think and learn together, things
can get unpredictable.

The facilitator plays an important role in moving from an agenda
to a real, productive meeting. (For the purposes of this chapter, we will
refer to "the facilitator" with the assumption that the term can apply to
someone facilitating alone or with a colleague.) The word "facilitate"
comes from the French word "faciliter" (to make easy), which comes
from the Latin "facile" (easy). At the simplest level, the job of the facilitator is to make it easy to accomplish the meeting's purpose—or at
least easier than it would be without the facilitator. Note that the word
"facilitate" does not come from words that mean "to direct," "to always
know what's best," or "to do most of the talking."

By "easy," we do not mean that facilitators are doing the work of
the meeting and letting everyone else sit back and relax. "Easy" here
means that facilitators are helping the meeting run smoothly so that
participants' energy and attention are focused on the most important
business of the meeting. It is appropriate for participants to feel challenged by the exchange of ideas and the weight of the objectives, but

not for them to feel confused by a lack of clarity about purpose, process, or next steps.

While the facilitator's job is to make accomplishing the goals of the meeting easy, that does not mean the facilitator's task is easy. Facilitators are simultaneously keeping an eye on both content and process, on both the objectives and the experience of the participants along the way. They make multiple micro-decisions throughout the meeting, including when and how to adjust course and when to hold steady, all the while supporting full engagement, managing conflict, and being aware of their role and influence.

Sound overwhelming? It doesn't have to be. There are some very concrete things—we call them "top tips"—that facilitators can do during a meeting to make it productive (see Exhibit 5.1). Since responsibility for making a meeting go well does not rest entirely with the

Exhibit 5.1

Top Tips for Facilitators	
TASK	**TOP TIPS**
1 Keeping to (and Deviating from) the Agenda	• Start on time • Let purpose rule • Clarify next steps and decision processes • Listen to feedback • End on time
2 Supporting Full Engagement	• Welcome participants • Clarify roles • Check on preparation • Make room for many voices • Use visual tools
3 Managing Conflict	• Set the tone • Review norms
4 Maintaining Awareness of the Role You Play	• Choose your seat deliberately • Model being a learner

facilitator, we have also identified a separate, complementary list of top tips for *participants*, which we describe in chapter 6.

As you read chapter 5, keep your facilitator hat on as you take in the top tips for facilitators for each of the four actions shown in the table. And get ready to switch to your participant hat for chapter 6. We know better than to suggest that our top tips alone will guarantee success. Meetings can and do get messy, which is why we follow each set of tips by naming several common dilemmas and offering ideas about what to do when they arise. The dilemmas for facilitators are shown in Exhibit 5.2; the dilemmas for participants are listed in chapter 6.

In this chapter, we will go through the four key actions and look at top tips and common dilemmas for each.

Exhibit 5.2

Common Dilemmas for Facilitators	
TASK	**DILEMMA**
1 Keeping to (and Deviating from) the Agenda	• You're not ready at start time • The conversation wanders • A new topic comes up • An agenda item is taking too long • You can't finish on time
2 Supporting Full Engagement	• There's silence • The activity isn't working • You're too much at the center of things • There's an energy lull • Some or all people are participating virtually
3 Managing Conflict	• People don't know how to disagree • Norms are violated • One person is the problem • The culture is the problem • You're uncomfortable
4 Maintaining Awareness of the Role You Play	• You have less authority than others • You have more authority than others

TASK 1: KEEPING TO (AND DEVIATING FROM) THE AGENDA

The irony of very carefully designing an agenda is that you can end up quite invested in getting through it all. But if you have been successful in fully engaging participants in wrestling with important topics, the meeting is almost guaranteed to generate a discussion so lively that keeping to the agenda feels hard to do.

Part of the art of facilitating is deciding when to stay with the carefully crafted agenda and when to depart from it, and how to do either one. You may have a personal preference that guides your decision making. That is true for the two of us—Kathy defaults to keeping to the agenda, while Liz is more inclined to adjust in the moment. However, both of us do our best to follow as many of our own "top tips" as context will allow, so that we are well positioned to deal with the dilemmas around staying the course or adjusting midstream that inevitably arise.

Top Tips

START ON TIME You set a start time when you made your agenda; as facilitator, it is your job to stick to it. Doing so increases the likelihood that you will achieve the meeting's objectives. Perhaps even more important, in the long run, it helps create a culture in which people feel that their time is valued. Part of building trust is doing what you said you were going to do and then showing people that you're going to use their time well. This is true especially in cultures where "nothing" starts on time. Your meeting still can, and people will appreciate that.

A key to starting *on time* is having the facilitator arrive *early*. Even a few minutes can make an enormous difference in your ability to transition to the present moment—and help everyone else do the same. Kathy used to swoop into most meetings, breathless from the little thrill of adrenaline that comes from having the elevator make every local stop just when she most needed an express. When she started putting on her calendar that she needed to be in the room well ahead of time, things changed. Now there is time to check on the room and technology setup, review the agenda and its purpose, and enjoy a little unscheduled chatting time with participants. Early arrivals are happy to pitch in and help with furniture moving and handout distribution, which creates a feeling of shared ownership of the success of the meeting.

The other key to an on-time start, of course, is having participants be there when you need them. In our experience, if people know the start time is real, they honor that by being on time when they can and slipping in late when they can't. However, if people know the meeting rarely starts on time, many people (including us!) will make less of an effort to be there exactly on time. This leaves the facilitator to decide when enough people are there to corral folks into starting the meeting, and the people who were on time to wonder why the bothered to arrive at the appointed hour.

LET PURPOSE RULE In a wise meeting, the objectives are clearly stated at the top of the agenda and the facilitator opens by placing those particular objectives in the context of the broader goals that the team—and the organization more broadly—are working toward. For example, in the Greenville fifth-grade team example from chapter 3, lead teacher Rose might say at the beginning of the meeting:

> We've been trying to take on lots of things in our meetings, and we've discussed how it's hard to make progress on anything. Today, as you can see in the agenda, we're going to try to focus and go deeper. We've been working a lot on writing for the last several months, but haven't made the time to see whether and how our efforts are working for kids. So today we're going to look at the student writing prompts you've brought and discuss what we see, and we're going to decide how we might adjust our instruction. Then in future meetings, we'll see how our adjustments are going and figure out what we want to focus on for our next inquiry cycle.

As the meeting unfolds, the facilitator needs to keep the purpose in mind, using it as a North Star that reorients the group should they wander off. When the timekeeper announces that it is time to move on from a particular activity, facilitator and participants alike may feel interrupted. But this is a great opportunity for the facilitator to evaluate whether the conversation under way is indeed in service of the meeting objectives and greater purpose. If so, it may warrant using some more time to bring the discussion to a better stopping point. If not, the group is saved by the bell. Keeping a relentless focus on time helps ensure that, if the group gets a little sidetracked, you won't stay lost for long.

Continuing with the example of Greenville's fifth-grade team meeting, suppose that while looking at student writing, the group got sucked into a discussion about the speech challenges of a particular student. "I think we're getting too deep into the weeds here" can be a helpful comment to signal to the group that it is time to pull back and reorient toward the meeting's purpose.

At the end of the meeting, the facilitator can highlight how upcoming meetings will help move the team or organization forward within the broader purpose. For example, Rose might say:

> Now that we've looked at our data and identified some places where our instruction is working and not working, we've identified some adjustments to make in our classrooms. When we meet in two weeks, we'll observe how those adjustments are going, and we can decide then whether we want to continue with writing or switch to a new topic for our inquiry cycle. That will put us in good shape to report out in the whole-faculty meeting at the end of the month about how our work is contributing to the school-wide efforts around improving literacy.

CLARIFY NEXT STEPS AND DECISION PROCESSES As you move from one agenda item to the next, resist the temptation to leave things open-ended because you're short of time or reluctant to make the group commit. Our experience is that ambiguity almost invariably leaves work in the facilitator's lap later or means that little movement happens on the agenda item, since the group didn't resolve what to do next. Summarize where you think the group is stopping and what the next steps are; for example, "It sounds like we're committing to each doing X between now and the next meeting" or "I'm hearing two unresolved big questions [state the questions], and a desire to think more about those before we decide what to do. Who would be willing to meet to think about those questions and bring some ideas to our next meeting?"

In small work group meetings, it can be helpful to enter next steps into the meeting notes as soon as they are mentioned. Using a consistent format such as "[Name] will do [task] by [date]" can ensure that there is no confusion around who is doing what and by when.

When it is time to check in about whether a particular item was done, a next step that reads "Barbara and David will draft a rubric for the writing assignment by next Tuesday" is more useful than one phrased as "make a draft rubric."

If you find a dearth of volunteers to take on next steps, there are things you can do to make sure the follow-up work is shared. For example, allow more wait time when asking, ask people directly either before or during the meeting if they will take a hand (most people will say "yes" when put on the spot), or say that you'll follow up after the meeting to recruit.

When next steps involve the group making complex decisions, it is important to be clear about what the decision-making process is going to be. Are you deciding by consensus? Does that mean everyone has to agree, or just be able to live with the decision? Are you voting? Does your process vary depending on what you're deciding? See the Selected Protocols section of this book for some examples of decision-making protocols that we use in our meetings.

Our experience is that most groups don't mind (or at least can accept) when they're not *the* decision makers—but they do mind when there's uncertainty or vagueness about who actually is making the decision and what the role of the group is related to that decision. Explain how recommendations made by the group will roll up to decision makers and what the time frame is for decision making. Otherwise, meetings can feel either superfluous or downright disempowering—neither of which supports an effort to shift to a more collaborative culture in your organization.

LISTEN TO FEEDBACK If you answered "yes" to question 7 on the Meeting Wise Checklist, then you built time into your agenda for assessment of what worked and what didn't in the meeting (see the Plus/ Delta Protocol in the Resources section for instructions about one way to assess). As facilitator, your job during this reflection time is to review the original objectives of the meeting and acknowledge shifts to the agenda that may have occurred. Then invite comments that are specific to *content* (the extent to which the objectives were met) or to *process* (the extent to which the chosen activities as enacted supported the work). As participants offer feedback, listen carefully. Resisting the very human urge to explain or justify your decisions will make it less likely that you come across as defensive and will make it much easier for people to offer critical feedback. Expectation of an immediate rebuttal or explanation may make participants less likely to volunteer a suggestion. Acknowledge the comments with a simple "thank you," a clarification if necessary, such as "What I'm hearing is X. Is that right? Could you say a little more about that?" or a gentle probe, "What could we do to improve that next time?"

If participants are hesitant to provide suggestions, remind them that feedback will help the team improve its practice. That takes the focus off critiquing your performance as a facilitator. You can also prime the pump by offering an idea of your own or by allowing people to share their ideas with a partner. This can generate energy and confidence around articulating how the meeting could have been more effective.

The most effective strategy for encouraging candid feedback is opening each meeting by describing how you have adjusted the agenda to take into account the feedback you have received. Once participants see how seriously their feedback is taken, they are likely to become regular—and enthusiastic—contributors of ideas that help fine-tune the way the group uses collaborative time.

Finally, if you are short on time or believe that anonymous feedback would be most helpful, you can invite people to write their ideas on index cards or sticky notes and drop them off as they walk out the door. Whatever you do, don't skip this rich opportunity for improvement. If it was important enough to include on your agenda, it is important enough to make sure you do it on the day of the meeting.

END ON TIME A timely finish is just as important as a prompt start for signaling respect for the time of everyone in the meeting. If the end time is ambiguous, then there's less reason within the meeting to use time purposively and to make careful, if hard, trade-offs about time.

We like to wrap things up by thanking the group for their participation and stating that the formal meeting is over. We'll often accompany this with a visual signal such as standing up and closing a computer or notebook. When possible, we like to stick around for 15 minutes or so after the meeting to connect with participants and tidy up things on our computers and in the room. This informal extension can help dispel any sense of breathlessness that can accompany the intense concentration that comes with working hard throughout the meeting to make wise decisions about when to stick with or deviate from the agenda as written.

Common Dilemmas

Once a meeting begins, it is easy for the best-laid plans to go astray. Time can slip, objectives can shift, and people can wander. What's a facilitator to do?

WHEN YOU'RE NOT READY AT START TIME Our top tip is to start on time. But what if you're not able to? Should you forge ahead or wait a few minutes? The answer depends on what's holding you up. For sure, the furniture needs to be set up, but it may be OK to start if the technology is not working yet. If you have a co-facilitator, often one of you can get the meeting going while the other continues the preparation. If essential setup in not in place, then it's worth it to wait a few minutes and tell everyone, "We just need a little more time to get everything in order. We'll get started in X minutes." That honors people's time by allowing them to take care of something else if they want, or simply to know when their attention will be required.

What if someone important is not at the meeting yet? Perhaps it's the person taking the lead on the first agenda item, or a person with some authority. Ideally, you start without that person, since other people are there on time and ready to go and it is your responsibility to make good use of their time. You can begin by reviewing the agenda and objectives, and then perhaps shift another agenda item to the top if the first item is dependent on a particular person or you don't want to discuss it if that person is missing. If you do wait, let participants know you are doing that and why: "We're going to wait a few minutes for Holly to arrive because she has important background knowledge for our main agenda item." "We're going to wait a few minutes for the superintendent because we know he's coming from something else and doesn't want to miss this." In this situation, you may want to insert an impromptu check-in by asking people to turn and talk with a neighbor about a highlight of their day or week. Or you could invite people to review their preparation materials alone or in pairs, which can be a great way of helping people transition into the work at hand and warm up for a rich discussion once the meeting is under way.

WHEN THE CONVERSATION WANDERS When the conversation wanders from the agenda topic to something related but off track, the facilitator can help by reconnecting to purpose and refocusing the group's attention. An open-ended way to do that is to ask, "What's the connection between [that point] and [our purpose/topic]?" Sometimes people will respond to that question by making a connection that's not obvious to you, and sometimes they won't be able to make much of a connection, which shows them (and everyone else) that the conversation is off track. Another version of inviting connections is to ask the whole group to build from the current discussion back to shared purpose. For example, when facilitating the meeting described in the Greenville fifth-grade team example in chapter 3, Rose might say to a colleague, "That's a really interesting point about that particular student. How does that help us think about how our action plan for improving student writing is going?" Notice that Rose also incorporated a little validation ("really interesting point") to signal that it was a worthwhile observation while making sure the group didn't get sidetracked from its main purpose.

Another way to help a conversation get back on track is to summarize and provide checkpoints along the way. Facilitators play a key summarizing role, whether they do it themselves or invite participants to summarize. For example: "So far, what I'm hearing is a lot of enthusiasm for the idea, but a couple of key concerns as well. The concerns seem centered on whether we can add anything else to our already full plates and whether we'll have the support we need. Does that capture where we are? What did I miss?" or "We've put a lot of ideas on the table. Would someone be willing to try to summarize the main ideas?"

The key is remembering the top tip to let purpose be your North Star. If you're not clear on the most important thing you are trying to accomplish, no one else in the meeting will be either. Then the conversation is likely to achieve either (1) something different than the most important thing or (2) very little.

WHEN A NEW TOPIC COMES UP A variation of wandering is that a new topic arises. In wandering, the conversation started on track but evolved to a different, usually unclear place. A new topic, however, represents a clear break from the agenda. Participants might introduce new topics for a host of reasons, some noble (such as providing new context that the group needs to know in order to work productively) and some less so (such as attempting to take over the meeting to serve another purpose). When the conversation wanders, the facilitator's job is to help the group re-find the trail it's supposed to be on. When a new topic is introduced, the facilitator helps the group decide whether to take the new pathway or stick with the planned route.

If you've worked hard to create a thoughtful agenda, is it ever OK to change the primary purpose during the meeting? Our answers to most questions that begin with "Is it OK . . . ?" are "It depends" and "Think about *why* you would do one thing versus another and what the trade-offs are." If you're clear on why and make a decision with your eyes wide open about trade-offs, then go for it. But changing objectives during a meeting is a big decision that must be made quickly. Here are a few things to think about in the moment:

- **Why would you change the objective?** Because the person who's the loudest or has the most authority is suggesting it? (That's not a reason that's going to resonate with most of the meeting participants . . .) Because of new information that has emerged? Because of a change of context? For another reason? How compelling is that reason?

- **What are the trade-offs if you change the objective?** Will you gain trust by being responsive, or lose trust because people expected and prepared for one thing, and you're doing another (or some of both)? Will changing course this time mean that people will be less likely to prepare for the next meeting? The answer probably depends on whether there's any pattern around sticking to or changing objectives. If meetings frequently don't go as planned, people are less likely to be invested in any particular meeting or to prepare, whereas if a significant change is unusual, people are more likely to consider it an exception and appreciate the decision to change objectives.

- **How essential is it to address this new objective in order to meet the other objectives?** For example, in a meeting to "design the structure of the network," you may find in the course of the meeting that there is little consensus around who the network is going to serve. When you make a discovery like that, by all means adjust course. You are unlikely to make much progress toward your primary purpose if you do not have a common understanding from which to build.

Many groups find it helpful to have a place to record topics that come up but aren't relevant or can't be addressed in this particular meeting. A common technique is to use a "parking lot," which can take the form of chart paper posted on a wall or an open and shared online document. This practice allows people to name topics and "park" them somewhere else for future consideration (for example, "I know this isn't what we're talking about today, but I'd like to put this in the parking lot for a future discussion"), or for groups to acknowledge a new topic and stay focused on the topic at hand (for example, "That sounds important, but I don't think we have time to take that up well today. How about if we put that in the parking lot?").

Our one caution is to use the parking lot judiciously and to circle back to it. Otherwise, as we know from personal experience, there can be a lot of abandoned vehicles in the lot, and "parking lot" becomes a synonym for "We're not ever going to talk about this but it helps us move on right now to write it down." Be careful what you put in the parking lot in the first place—not every topic that arises needs to go there—and make sure to return to it to decide which topics to take up when. When Liz was a school principal, the faculty had generated so many things to discuss "later" that they declared one meeting to be "Later Day," and used it to address all the things they had been putting off. That worked well for miscellaneous topics, but sometimes things in the parking lot are big or contentious issues, and they may need a meeting of their own to be taken up well.

WHEN AN AGENDA ITEM IS TAKING TOO LONG When creating the agenda, the time you allotted to each activity was your best guess about how long the activity should take (see question 10 on the Meeting Wise Checklist). But what if you guessed wrong? When the agenda item is taking "too long," it may be that it is actually taking exactly as long as it needs to. How do you know? Do you stick with this agenda item or move on? Who gets to decide?

As with all of your decisions as a facilitator, keep the purpose of the meeting in mind. Is getting further with this agenda item key to the purpose of the meeting, or is an upcoming agenda item even more essential? If your answer is "both," perhaps you can take a little more time on this item and then move on. Or you can consider what could be done outside this meeting to finish up the item in question. Can a small group follow up between meetings? What agenda items really need the whole group's attention?

You can also think about how meetings connect to one another. For example, Rose on the Greenville fifth-grade team might say, "We're having a really interesting conversation about the writing prompts. But we had said we wanted to get to deciding how we will adjust our instruction. If we don't take that step, we might run out of time to do another full inquiry cycle before the end of the year."

While this is all going on in your head, you also have to figure out who gets to decide whether to adjust the agenda. Are you going to take meeting time to invite the group to give opinions or permission to adjust the agenda (when you're already behind!), or are you going to make the decision yourself and forge ahead? Kathy tends to make a call and tell participants about the adjustment; Liz likes to err on the side of engaging participants in decision making. In small meetings where there is a shared commitment to keeping close track of time, both of us have been known to say, "We built a 10-minute time bank into our agenda. Should we dip into the bank to allow us more time on this activity?"

An efficient way to deal with an agenda item that is taking more time than planned is to offer a proposal both about how much time to add and where to subtract it from. For example, "I think we could get to a good stopping point on this with a few more minutes. Would anyone object to us spending five more minutes on this? I think we could take the time out of our last agenda item. If necessary, we can push that item until next meeting." In this approach, if people really object, they can still say so because you've made your intentions clear, but they're unlikely to object unless they feel really strongly.

One of our guiding principles is that the more significant a shift is, the more important it is to invite the group to participate in making the decision about how to use time. If an item on the agenda is potentially going to get delayed or eliminated because of the choice you're about to make, it's worth inviting the group to weigh in, both because they'll bring valuable perspectives and because you're trying to create a culture of shared responsibility for meeting objectives.

The key to knowing what to do when an agenda item runs over time is to consciously and deliberately decide to break the rules and to engage participants in the decision making when possible. Nobody in the meeting (especially the facilitator!) should be surprised when time runs out before you get to one or more agenda items. That should be a deliberate choice made in the service of the meeting's purpose.

WHEN YOU CAN'T FINISH ON TIME If you have planned a wise meeting, then you said "yes" to the last question on the Meeting Wise Checklist because you were confident that it was realistic that you could get through the agenda in the time allocated. But once you're in the meeting, you might realize that you should have checked "no."

When, despite your best efforts, the meeting is running over the allotted time and it is not possible to wait until a future meeting to finish up, the first thing you need to do is *acknowledge that you are aware that time is up.* You can bet that other participants have noticed this, too, so just say so and avoid having others in the room worrying if they should let you know.

If you can do it sincerely, give people permission to leave; this helps build trust that you are truly valuing people's time. You could then ask who can stay; for example, "We are at the end of our scheduled time. If you need to leave, please do so. Is anyone able to stay for another X minutes to finish up?" We try to make it easy for people to leave unapologetically if they need to. After all, they've honored their commitment to the group by staying until the agreed-upon end time, and they may have other important, inflexible commitments afterward. If we don't create this opportunity, we lose even more time as individuals justify or apologize for their exits one by one, which can make the meeting go that much longer for everyone.

When the meeting is really over, we thank the people who could stay for giving extra time. Sometimes we also note that we made an extra withdrawal from the shared time bank, and promise to give people that time back in another meeting. For example, we might end another meeting five minutes early if we ran five minutes over in this meeting. While hard to do, this practice earns lots of goodwill from the group.

TASK 2: SUPPORTING FULL ENGAGEMENT

While you are trying to enact your carefully crafted agenda and figure out whether and when to adjust it, you're trying at the same time to pay attention to who's engaged, who's not, and how you know, since not all "engagement" is verbal. Part of the role of the facilitator is to make it easier for people to participate in a variety of ways. If participants' full engagement *isn't* required, why have them at the meeting in the first place? And as long as they're at the meeting, why not engage them so that they can contribute to the meeting's purpose and so that the meeting can contribute to their learning?

Top Tips

WELCOME PARTICIPANTS Before the meeting starts, greet people as they come in. Notice how they enter: Do they seem particularly happy about something? Do they seem upset? Distracted? If the meeting is not too large, saying hello and welcoming each person by name (or introducing yourself if you don't know them) can help people bring their attention to the moment and appreciate that their presence is valued.

Let people know if there is anything to do before the meeting starts, such as making a name tag, picking up handouts, or getting a cup of coffee. If as part of your preparation you assigned seats or put people into groups, or if you have other directions around seating, it is efficient to put instructions on a screen or chart paper. A simple note like "Please sit with people you don't know well" or "Sit in groups of four" can help folks get situated efficiently. This is a small thing that helps alleviate the confusion of people trying to find their place or figure out where they're supposed to be, and also relieves you of the pressure of telling everyone something individually.

If someone comes in after the meeting has started, welcome that person, too. Use your judgment about how best to do that. If the meeting is in a whole-group discussion, we tend to welcome late arrivals publicly if it won't be too disruptive to the group at that moment. Other times, we'll simply make eye contact with the new arrival and offer a smile to acknowledge their presence, which lets them slip in less obtrusively (something we know we appreciate when we have to arrive late somewhere). Either way, sometimes we'll offer one sentence out loud about where we are in the meeting, such as "We're reviewing the objectives" or "We're discussing the first agenda item and have just heard a few different ideas, which include . . ."

The trick is to balance getting the new arrival oriented and ready to participate with not wasting the time of the people who arrived on time. Depending on where you are in the meeting, a quick summary of where you are can be useful to everyone, not just the new arrival. If the meeting is working in small groups when someone arrives late, it's much easier. Greet new arrivals one-on-one and either catch them up quickly on what's happened so far and what the current activity is, or invite another participant to do that.

CLARIFY ROLES People will be best able to engage if they know how you expect them to participate. Ideally, people who have formal roles, like timekeeper and note taker, know what is expected of them ahead of time (see chapter 2 for a discussion of roles). Sometimes, however, roles aren't preassigned, or you want to make sure everyone knows what the role entails, so it is helpful to spend a few minutes at the beginning of the meeting enlisting and clarifying. For example, "We need a timekeeper today. Who would be willing to do that? . . . Thank you, Khita. If you could keep an eye on time and let us know when we have three minutes before time is up for each agenda item, that would be great. You may want to set an alarm that everyone can hear; that way you won't have to try to find a convenient place to interrupt." Or "Note taker, your role is to capture key decisions and next steps. Don't worry about capturing everything that's being said." Doing this out loud authorizes the person to play a particular role at the same time that it clarifies the role. More unusual roles like "next step tracker" might also need some clarification. In particular, you'll need to explain whether you want the person to flag next steps as they come up, confirming the nature of the task, who will do it, and by when, or whether you want the person to share the complete list of next steps at the end of the meeting, at which time volunteers and deadlines can be set.

It is also good to offer clarity for more general roles you may want people to play; for example, "Today we'll be reviewing our draft proposal before sending it to the chancellor. If you see a weakness in our argument, don't hold back. We are relying on you all to act as critical friends." Or "I hope returning members will take this opportunity to make new folks feel welcome in our community, and that everyone will jump in with questions as they arise."

And finally, it can be helpful to clarify how you see your role as facilitator: "My job is to help us accomplish the objectives on our agenda. I'll do that by monitoring our process and trying to help bring us back to the objectives if we stray off course. I'll be counting on you to keep our objectives top of mind as well."

CHECK ON PREPARATION Your agenda may have clearly specified the pre-work for participants. But did they actually do it? The answer to this question will have a substantial impact on how people can engage in the meeting. The trick here is to check in a safe way, since few people like to admit that they're unprepared. We usually provide an opportunity at the beginning of the meeting for people to "come clean" if they are not prepared so that they don't spend the meeting trying to *pretend* that they are.

We try to focus on the meeting rather than on the people. For example, instead of saying, "Who didn't do the reading?" we might say something like, "Before we dive in, it would be really helpful if we knew who was able to do the reading and who wasn't. We're going to be relying heavily on the reading, so if you weren't able to do it, we'll find some other ways for you to contribute." Sometimes we'll ask who *was* able to do it, which makes it a little less embarrassing for unprepared people, but harder on the facilitator to tell who is in the "didn't" category.

Doing this check-in helps you know whether enough people are prepared to proceed. If a lot of people aren't prepared, we sometimes will invite someone who is prepared to give a summary, or we will give the whole group time to prepare in the meeting. Those are both suboptimal because they reinforce that people don't really need to prepare in advance, but if that content is essential for today, we'll acknowledge the people who did prepare and make clear that the only reason we're taking meeting time to prepare is that we need everyone's voices included for this important discussion.

When only a few people are unprepared, you can offer different roles or time to catch up. Examples of alternative roles include norms checker or summarizer of the discussion, both of which allow a person to make a meaningful contribution without knowing the content. If it's essential that they prepare this content right now, give them time to catch up out in the hallway or in some other way that doesn't distract from the meeting.

We've found that the single biggest motivator for doing required prep work is the knowledge that the preparation will be well used during the meeting. By drawing on the pre-work consistently, you both reward those who did prepare and encourage those who didn't to do so next time.

MAKE ROOM FOR MANY VOICES In a typical meeting, uneven participation is common. Often, one or two people do most of the talking, several people are quiet, and everyone else is somewhere in between. As facilitator, there are several things you can do to break this typical pattern. But remember: the goal is not to get everyone speaking an equal amount, but to engage everyone and use that engagement to achieve your collective purpose. Remember also that people bring different strengths and preferences, and part of your task is to capitalize on those so that everyone makes a meaningful contribution.

If one or two people are dominating (often the fastest thinkers or people who like to process by talking; sometimes people with the most power or people who feel particularly strongly about an issue), your challenge is to make room for other voices in the conversation. To do this, you may want to specifically invite people who haven't spoken yet to join in, perhaps with a new prompt. For example, "We've heard some ideas about how to involve parents in developing a growth mindset. What are some of the other things you've tried or considered? Let's hear first from people who haven't had a chance to get in on the conversation." Usually, the talkative people will try to hold their tongues until at least a couple of other people have spoken.

Another approach is to give everyone time to turn and talk with a neighbor—or "pair-share"—about an issue before discussing it in the whole group. This approach lets the talkative people do their processing with a colleague and be heard, and lets the quieter folks gather their thoughts so they can feel more prepared to talk in the whole group. We use this technique frequently, even when we haven't planned it ahead of time. If we notice that a few people are dominating the conversation, we might switch to a pair-share for a few minutes. Then, when we come back to the whole group, we give the cue to hear first from people we haven't heard from yet, or we start with a few pairs who haven't said much: "Zöe and Ana, what's something that came out of your conversation?"

A variation of the pair-share is the *think*-pair-share, in which you invite everyone to think for a moment and then turn and talk. Related variations are to invite everyone to *write* and then turn and talk, or to go straight from writing to whole group discussion. All of these approaches enrich the conversation by encouraging quieter voices and by making space for everyone to be more thoughtful.

If there are particular people you want to hear more from or less from (either generally or about a specific topic on the agenda), it can be helpful to "pre-wire" or connect with those people before the meeting or during a break. That might be as simple as encouraging someone just before the meeting—"I'm really looking forward to what you have to say about the new proposal today"—or may involve a separate meeting—"James, I noticed that in our last meeting you spoke about twice as much as anyone else. You're adding a lot to the meeting, but we're also missing hearing from other people. How might we be able to work together to create more opportunities for other people to contribute?"

Also in the meeting, you can assign roles for activities; for example, you could have the person with the longest middle name lead each breakout session, or the person with the birthday closest to today to be the one who shares out. This approach introduces a fun and random element that usually yields a mix of voices.

And finally, rather than being the one who tries to moderate who's participating when, you can let participants call on each other, either by name or by having each person who speaks be responsible for tossing a ball to the next speaker. Groups often self-regulate participation pretty well—and more easily than the facilitator. And letting people call on each other makes participation the responsibility of the whole group.

USE VISUAL CUES AND TOOLS Another way to make room for many voices is to have a visual way to share talk time. For example, some groups use a "talking stick" or some other tangible object like a ball, and only the person holding the object can talk. While this can make it harder to have a conversation that builds in a logical way, it can also make it easier to share the floor. A variation of this approach is to have a number of small objects that act as talk tokens. Each person gets the same allotment, and each time a person talks, he or she spends a token. Once people are out of tokens, they're out of talk turns until the other participants have spent theirs. Again, this can feel a little unnatural or stilted, but it usually does make people consider carefully before they talk about whether what they have to say is worth spending a token on. There is something about the visual that helps remind each person how much he or she has spoken, and makes it easier for the group to see who hasn't spoken much and who has spoken a lot.

You can also use public note taking to keep people focused and to reduce repetitive comments. You can ask people to add to what is not already on the board; if something they agree with is already noted, they can add a check mark. Or you can ask someone who has a knack for visual representation to sketch ideas where everyone can see them. We try to hold meetings in rooms where there is a whiteboard, and often end meetings with having someone take a picture of our sketches and send them around to the group. Drawing often captures the non-linear quality of a conversation better than notes alone ever could.

Common Dilemmas

Some of the most common challenges a facilitator faces are about participation—too much, too little. Below are several suggestions for how to help participation be "just right."

WHEN THERE'S SILENCE When the room gets quiet, the first thing to know is that it feels a lot longer to you than it actually is. You can test this by actually timing it, or you can make yourself count to "10 Mississippi" before speaking. Keep in mind that silence is OK. It often means people are thinking. And thinking is good. It's called "wait time" for a reason. You are waiting for someone else to speak, not you. Three seconds is not wait time. Only the fastest thinkers and talkers are going to chime in within the first three seconds. And there may be some 10-second thinkers who will add a lot to the conversation.

To help yourself wait, doodle on your agenda. Remind the group that silence is OK and that you're good at wait time, which tells the group you're not going to rescue them. Sing to yourself or write your own response to the topic at hand. And if you do all that, and it's still quiet, you can either invite people to turn and talk with a neighbor or you can check in with the group. "Why is it quiet? Are you think-ing? Confused? Not interested in this topic?" Often, when you inquire, people might tell you that they're not clear on what you're asking them to do or there's something simmering beneath the surface that no one wants to name. Or maybe they do just need more time to process.

Sometimes people are silent because they're having trouble keep-ing track of the conversation. In these cases, oral summaries can help, and visual tools (see our top tip on this point) can be even more helpful. For example, write the three options being discussed or ask someone in the group to record the brainstorm in a place where the participants can see it instead of having to rely on their memories.

WHEN THE ACTIVITY ISN'T WORKING Despite your best advance planning and your attempts at adjustments during the meeting, sometimes an activity just isn't working. It falls flat or is not helping the group make progress on the objectives.

When an activity isn't working well, one option is to let it run its course (or even end early) and move on to the next activity. Get feed-back at the end of the meeting and improve it for next time. This is a sensible option if the activity has been good enough to help on the objectives, even if it has not been great, or if the time it would take to make a significant shift isn't likely to be worth the potential improve-ment during this meeting.

Another option is to seek help privately to figure out what to do. This is one of the times when co-facilitators can be particularly sup-portive. If you don't have a co-facilitator and there are other people who might be helpful, tap into one of them for a private check-in. Huddle during a break or when participants are talking in small groups (you may need to insert an impromptu pair-share or writing activity to cre-ate space for this). Invite their opinions on why the current activity isn't working. Often they will have noticed something you haven't, or have other ideas about what to try.

A third option is to enlist help more publicly. Invite participants to help figure out what's happening and how to get unstuck. For example, you might say, "It feels like we're talking in circles or rehashing the same ideas. Why is that? What might help us go deeper?" You might also take a break and make an open invitation for consults: "It feels like this isn't getting us where we need to go, and I'm not sure how to get there. Let's take a 10-minute break. If anyone has some thoughts about why we're stuck or what to do about it, I'd really appreciate hearing from you during break." This particular option has the advantage of sharing the responsibility of fruitful participation across the group, though it also takes more time to make an adjustment.

WHEN YOU'RE TOO MUCH AT THE CENTER OF THINGS If the group is relying too heavily on you, they won't be participating fully. And you'll probably be very tired when the meeting is over. One way to tell if this is happening is to picture drawing the pattern of interaction. If it goes facilitator-participant-facilitator-participant, it will look a lot like a wheel with you at the hub.

To help you avoid taking the hub (or having participants put you there), a variety of tactics can deflect attention from yourself. For example, ask open-ended questions and wait for responses. Close-ended questions are like a boomerang that comes right back at you quickly as people wait for you to ask the next question or make the next move. You can also take notes on who's talking or not and what's being said, which can both be useful to you and let you break eye contact with the group. Lack of eye contact from you encourages people to both look at and talk with one another. You can also choose to make eye contact to encourage people to speak, either by looking at a specific person or looking around the group. More subtly, take a drink of water, reach for something in your bag, or rest your chin on your hand and cover your mouth while listening. All of these tactics send signals that you're not going to talk and thus encourage others to do so.

You can also be transparent about trying to get yourself out of the center of things: "Try talking with each other, not to me. I might not look at you. I'm still listening, but am trying to encourage you to talk with each other." Or, during the conversation, you might say, "A lot of the comments and questions seem to be directed at me. This is our collective conversation, so try posing a question to the group or addressing one another." Or, if a comment or question is directed at you, turn it back over to the group: "What do other people think about that?"

When we find ourselves feeling reluctant to give up center stage, we think about whose needs we're serving. Our own need to feel important and valuable? The group's need to have someone else take responsibility? Or our shared need to meet the objectives? We also think carefully about how to put challenges back on the group. How can we sit back and let the group figure something out rather than jumping in and asking a question or offering a next step? Remember that doing nothing can be powerful when it leaves more space for the group to work things out on its own.

WHEN THERE'S AN ENERGY LULL A low-energy group is usually not a high-productivity group. So keep your antennae out for energy lags. Are people slipping out of the room to take a break? Is the room getting quieter? Is the conversation slowing? Do people look droopy? Then do something! Here are a few ideas:

- **Take a break.** Even if it's not scheduled, take a break. A 5- or 10-minute break can make a big difference in energy level. Our rule of thumb is to try not to go longer than 90 minutes without some kind of break. If the whole meeting lasts only two hours, we might not take a break, but we'll keep an eye on the energy level to see if it's needed. If we have a longer break, we'll often encourage people to go outside and get some fresh air.

- **Get everyone talking.** Our favorite pair-share tactic comes in handy again here. Anything that gets everyone's voices in the room brings up the energy level and reengages everyone.

- **Shift the activity to include movement.** For example, instead of a report out, do a gallery walk (e.g., post ideas on chart paper and let people browse them like they're in a museum). That changes a sitting and listening activity into a walk and discuss ideas activity. Or, instead of getting people to turn and talk to a neighbor, invite them to get up and find someone they haven't talked with yet. Movement helps brains work better.

- **Have some fun.** A little bit of silliness can inject some energy into the room. Toss a ball for talk turns, or sing a song, play a game, or do some other quick energizer. See the Selected Protocols section of this book for some examples of energizers that we use in our meetings.

While all of these options take a little time, they also have big pay-off in the value of the remaining meeting time.

WHEN SOME OR ALL PEOPLE ARE PARTICIPATING VIRTUALLY Lots of meetings are conducted over the phone or via computers. While this can pose some unique challenges for facilitation, it is very possible to have a fabulous meeting without having everyone in the same space. When meetings are conducted in cyberspace, invite virtual participants in by name. This is an exception to our general stance of not calling on people in meetings and instead allowing them to choose when to talk. When people are participating virtually, it can be really hard for them to jump into the conversation, particularly but not exclusively when some people are meeting face to face and others are virtual. Sometimes we'll invite the virtual folks to weigh in first on a particular question or issue, and sometimes we'll pause and invite a particular virtual participants in by name: "André, what are your thoughts about this?"

TASK 3: MANAGING CONFLICT

Part of your job as a facilitator is to promote healthy conflict. By "healthy conflict," we mean productive disagreement about ideas in the service of the meeting's objectives. Our colleague Dick Murnane uses the imagery of heat and light. You want the kind of heat and disagreement in a meeting that sheds light and makes ideas better. Some of the most illuminating moments we've experienced in meetings have come from differences of opinion, perspective, or ideas that people have been comfortable and courageous enough to share. Many groups, particularly in education with its pervasive "culture of nice," are uncomfortable with conflict and thus have meetings with little heat and thus little light.

This section includes ideas for how to help a neutral meeting get a little hotter, how to bring light to a meeting that is dim, and how to help everyone in the meeting (including you) feel safe enough to stand closer to the heat.

Top Tips

REVIEW NORMS The facilitator's number-one job related to managing conflict is to make participants feel that it is safe to express their ideas. In chapter 4, we discussed the importance of setting group norms. The power of these norms, however, lies not in the act of setting them but in the frequency and care with which the group returns to them. If norms are visible within the meeting space, it is easy to reference them throughout the discussion. You can do this by posting them on chart paper or a board, by placing folded card stock with printed norms on each table, or by writing the norms right into the agenda for all to see.

As the meeting opens, remind people of the norms, referring back to any norm-related reflections from previous meetings; for example, "Last time, we said that we could do a better job challenging each other," or "We've identified careful listening as something that we want to get better at doing." Then invite people to set a group goal around improving adherence to a particular norm: "We're going to be talking about some pretty tough issues today, things that each of us may feel particularly strongly about. What would careful listening look like and sound like for us?" You can also invite individuals to set goals for their own participation (common ones we've seen are "Talk less," "Talk more," and "Assume positive intentions"). Write goals down so that you can return to them at the end of the meeting.

You can also have a role like "process checker" or "norms checker" focused on noticing and documenting how group dynamics are playing out. This can be particularly helpful if a group is struggling to uphold one or more of its norms or is early in learning to work together. For example, if a group norm is to share airtime, the process checker could keep a running tally of how many times each person in the room spoke and for how long. Viewing this quantitative data at the end of the meeting helps the group understand how they are functioning (and the very knowledge that the data is being collected might actually change the dynamic on the spot!). Though we often will ask for volunteers for this role, as we mentioned earlier in this chapter, this role can be a good one for someone who is unprepared for a meeting—that way they can contribute to the meeting in a different way. We often will have two norms checkers so that we get a variety of perspectives.

To close the meeting, invite the group to reflect on process: "How did we do with our norm around listening?" "Which of our norms did we follow most faithfully? Least faithfully? What's the evidence?" If you have norms checkers, have them start the reflection and then invite the rest of the group to add to the discussion.

SET THE TONE Promoting healthy conflict often requires more than a simple review of norms, however. Facilitators often need to remind participants as a series of meetings kicks off (and again as necessary at subsequent meetings) that disagreement is healthy and strengthens ideas. For example, in the Jackson County central office leadership team example from chapter 3, when introducing the new format for Monday morning meetings, Superintendent Nancy Cook might open by saying that she hopes participants will respectfully challenge one another's thinking as they offer solutions to the dilemmas presented. "We'll be putting our most challenging problems on the table. We need to be able to count on one another to look at them from many angles, and we need a real give-and-take around proposed solutions. As we do that, let's be hard on the substance, but soft on the people."[1]

Common Dilemmas

Conflict dilemmas run the gamut from no conflict to too much conflict to not the right kind of conflict to you feeling downright queasy about conflict. From the evidence you see, you have to quickly hypothesize and diagnose what the problem is and then decide what to do or not to do about it. This process of diagnosis and decision is at the heart of the facilitator's job throughout the meeting, and is particularly important with conflict because too much heat without light can be dangerous (while little heat and light can be both boring and unproductive).

WHEN PEOPLE DON'T KNOW HOW TO DISAGREE Sometimes the issue is that a group doesn't know how to disagree or isn't aware of its patterns. This can manifest itself as a very polite meeting or a meeting with disrespectful or heat-without-light moments. If the problem is awareness, track some data about interactions (you can also enlist participants to do this). How many disagreements or challenges to ideas were there? How many unanswered questions were there? How well did the group build on one another's ideas? Share the data at the end of the meeting and invite the group to reflect on it. If the problem is that the group doesn't know how to disagree productively, here are several ideas for how to help the group practice and learn:

- **Use the language of "heat and light."** We often deploy this language to give people an image of what we're aiming for: "Let's continue discussing this idea and remember that a little heat will often bring some light. Let's hear some alternative perspectives to bring some heat." Or, "The conversation is heating up, which could be really productive. Let's remember to keep the focus on ideas, not people, so that the heat brings light."

- **Role play.** Try authorizing people to disagree with each other by giving them roles outside their normal ones. The roles might be particular positions (e.g., "parent," "student," "teacher," "community member"), or might be process roles (e.g., "optimist," "questioner," "critic," "pragmatist," "devil's advocate"). Write the roles on index cards and have each person choose a card (your choice as to whether the person can decide on the role or whether it's random). Then have people take on that role for at least part of the discussion. You also can have people rotate roles partway through the discussion. An even simpler approach is to assign one group to give "pro" arguments on an issue and another to offer the "cons" even if those are not their true feelings. There is something about playing a role that authorizes people to disagree with one another more freely than if they speak as their actual selves. Sometimes people can take their role a little too far, at which point you could remind them to use it as an opportunity to practice healthy conflict, not take the stage.

- **Make it easy to disagree.** This a bit unnatural and takes practice as a facilitator, but can make a big difference: ask a question so that a "yes" or affirmative response is a dissent. For example, "Does anyone disagree with the proposal on the table?" instead of "Do you agree with the proposal?" or "Would anyone object if we extended this agenda item five more minutes?" instead of "Is everyone okay with us extending this agenda item?" It's easier to offer a response that sounds like a "yes," so by framing a "yes" as a dissent, you're making it easier for people to disagree. This subtle difference also makes it sound more like you're actually checking in rather than looking for endorsements of what you said.

- **Recognize and celebrate when healthy conflict happens.** A simple but powerful thing to do is to publicly name and reinforce when productive conflict happens. For example, you might say, "Ruth, that question you asked tested some important assumptions and helped us look at that issue again." or "Frank, thank you for sharing your discomfort with the way the conversation was headed. That took some courage. As you can see, once you opened up the possibility of disagreeing, we heard a much wider range of opinions." Make such acknowledgments in the moment or at the end of the meeting during debrief time.

These sorts of tactics can be deployed in any stage of a group's development. In some ways, it is harder when the group is newly formed because people are building trust and tend to tiptoe around disagreements until they know each other. In other ways, however, it is easier when a group is in early stages of formation because the members don't have habits around avoiding conflict yet. Whatever the group's stage of development, explicit naming and clarification of what productive disagreement looks like, sounds like, and feels like can help the group get better at it.

WHEN NORMS ARE VIOLATED   In chapter 4, we discussed how, when norms are violated, the *group* has to do something about it, not just the facilitator. If you have set the consequences in advance for violations of norms, the group may readily step in when needed. For example, we know of many groups where it is customary to start humming when someone makes a statement that is not backed up with evidence.

But what if a norms violation happens in the meeting and no one names it? We try to either give a general reminder or name it in as low-key a way as possible: "Let's watch our airtime so that we can hear from everyone"; "That sounded more like assuming the worst than assuming best intentions"; "Start on time/end on time applies to breaks, too, or we won't be able to keep to our norm of ending on time." That is usually enough to signal to the group and to the violator that you, at least, noticed and that the norm matters. It can be particularly helpful when *you* violate a norm to call yourself on it, especially with humor: "Oops . . . we have a norm to stick to protocol and I just spoke out of turn. I'm afraid I may need to start a support group on that one!"

Sometimes, however, a breach is so great that it feels wrong to make light of it. If you think someone is being or feeling attacked, it is important to acknowledge the situation, bringing it back to your own perception of what is going on: "I'm feeling like things are getting a little too hot in here, and there's a lot to process. Let's see if a five-minute break will help us return to this conversation productively."

WHEN ONE PERSON IS THE PROBLEM While it's rare that one person is *the* problem, it is true that one person can shift meeting dynamics considerably and can leave you at least inwardly frustrated as your various gentle tactics accomplish little. When this happens, we find it helpful to keep a few things in mind, and then try a few more deliberate tactics.

The first thing we try to keep in mind is something we learned from our colleagues Bob Kegan and Lisa Lahey, which is about what they call "the language of complaint." The basic idea is that complaints come from caring, so even if something sounds like a negative, not-so-productive comment, the root of it is usually something the person cares about deeply (and about which other people in the group probably care or at least respect). So remind yourself that complaints come from caring and to try to figure out what is it that this person cares about.

We also try to remind ourselves to focus more on what the person contributes to the group than on all the ways he or she is making our work as a facilitator difficult. People's strengths and challenges are often flip sides of the same coin. That person who always seems negative may also be the bravest one in the room and willing to name the difficult truths. A related reminder is to separate people from their behaviors, both in your own head and when talking to them or about them. Thus, it's not Jenna who drives you crazy, it's the way Jenna revisits decisions after they've been made.

And finally, we try to remind ourselves that it really is never just "one person" who's the problem. At minimum, the group is doing some combination of allowing and encouraging the person's behavior (no one else is naming difficult truths because the group is happy to let Carlos be the one who does that). All of these reminders get us in the right frame of mind to support the person in being a more productive member of the group. They also help us not send inadvertent signals during the meeting, like a sharp tone or an exasperated breath or a roll of the eyes.

Then, if a person is a significant disruption or negative force, we usually try to manage the behavior within the meeting itself and follow up between and during subsequent meetings with one of three approaches. We often start by going to the source. We talk with (and mostly listen to) the person and try to understand what the real issue is, which is not always the thing he or she was talking about in the meeting. This can give us both an earful *and* some better understanding of what was happening for that person in the meeting and what motivated the behavior.

Next, we try to invite disruptors to be part of the solution because we have some shared purpose but are going about it in different ways. We explain how, in our observation, the behavior affects the group's ability to move toward that purpose. We ask what we could do and what they could do to more productively move toward that the purpose. If this doesn't work, we enlist a colleague to talk with them before the meeting, or sit next to them during a meeting and help them monitor their behavior. And sometimes we find that *we're* the ones who need a buddy to help manage ourselves when our buttons get pushed.

WHEN THE CULTURE IS THE PROBLEM Sometimes the problem seems much more pervasive than one person. Maybe the culture is overly civil and "nice." Maybe people focus on problems outside the group's control rather than solutions within their control. Maybe people in the group don't seem to respect or like each other. These challenges are all bigger than one meeting. They have deeper roots, and they often reflect some of the dysfunctions of the larger organization or system in which this group is embedded. While a facilitator can't take on the overall organizational culture, that culture can be hard to ignore if it's affecting every meeting.

The suggestions above for setting the tone, intervening when norms are violated, and helping people learn how to disagree all are done within the context of a regular meeting. But sometimes we have found that we need to devote significant time to process and culture. That might mean spending some time helping people get to know each other as human beings (it's much harder to be disrespectful or assume worst intentions if you actually know someone).

Or it could mean naming and spending time on a larger conflict or simmering issue. The group may need to add a meeting to talk about a conflict that is bigger than the meeting objectives. Until the unnamed "it" that is getting in a group's way is addressed, making progress on meeting objectives could be impossible. In this situation, we enlist people in the group—and outside of it—to help us think about how to engage the conflict directly.

WHEN YOU'RE UNCOMFORTABLE Does conflict make you queasy? Are there certain topics that you're not sure how to handle? It's OK if you're uncomfortable—no doubt people in the group have a range of comfort and discomfort with the very topics you do. You are allowed to be human as a facilitator. That said, your discomfort can make it harder to facilitate, especially if you allow a conversation to get too hot because you're unsure how to intervene or are worried about how you'll be perceived by the group if you do.

One possibility is to make your own discomfort transparent to the group, which lets them know you're human, makes it easier for them to express discomfort, and makes them more likely to be your allies and to forgive you when you do something clumsy. You could say something like, "I don't know about you all, but this topic is hard for me to engage in. I feel uncomfortable and uncertain about how to proceed as soon as we start talking about X. I hope you'll help me, and I'll try to help the group have a productive conversation."

Another possibility is to be mindful of your own discomfort and try to correct for it during the meeting. If you know you're less likely to call someone on a norm violation, remind the group about norms before the discussion of the topic begins, or remind yourself to watch out for a particular norm. If something emerges unexpectedly and you're not sure what to do, again, you can be transparent about it either to the whole group or to a co-facilitator or colleagues during a break, "I'm not sure what to do here. What suggestions do you have?" Or you can simply do your best in the moment, invite the group to reflect at the end of the meeting, and perhaps offer your own reflection about what was hard or what you're thinking about now.

TASK 4: MAINTAINING AWARENESS OF THE ROLE YOU PLAY

As facilitator, you have an important role to play. You probably have more authority than you think you do (though likely not as much as you sometimes wish you had!). Keep in mind that what you choose to say and do will strongly influence the direction of the group. So choose wisely.

Top Tips

CHOOSE YOUR SEAT DELIBERATELY Unless we're sitting at a round table, one of the first things we ponder as enter a meeting room is where to sit. We usually opt for a place that's not the head of the table, but does let us see all the participants well, which is important for monitoring engagement. That said, sometimes the head of the table or the front of the room is the only place to see everyone well, so we sit there, knowing that it sends a signal about power that we may need to counterbalance with some other moves to invite full engagement.

MODEL BEING A LEARNER Throughout a meeting, know that what you *do* matters more than what you *say*. Modeling, including modeling making mistakes and being less than perfect, can be very powerful for helping the group learn how to grow together. One way to model that you're a learner (and not the omniscient presence some people might hope you to be or resent you for being) is to invite feedback on your facilitation. You might enlist a co-facilitator, colleague, or even the whole group in giving you feedback on something you are trying to improve. "I'm working on resisting the temptation to praise everyone's comments, so I may come across as less enthusiastic than usual today. Can you keep an eye on this and let me know at the end of the meeting if this approach leads to a richer conversation?"

And whenever you can, model that it is OK to not know something. When the facilitator can admit ignorance, it signals to the group that the task is to work together to seek knowledge and understanding.

Common Dilemmas

Sometimes the people who pay your salary or decide your future employment are the ones you are trying to gently corral. Other times you're facilitating a conversation among people who report to you or defer to you for other reasons. In either case, it can be helpful to acknowledge (but not get tripped up by) the nature of these relationships.

WHEN YOU HAVE LESS AUTHORITY THAN OTHERS It can be tricky if you're facilitating a meeting but don't have the most authority in the room. This is obvious if someone has more senior positional authority than you do, and is less obvious but also relevant if someone has particular informal authority or is a well-respected opinion leader in the group. As a rule of thumb, those people shouldn't be any more surprised in a meeting than you are. This often means talking with people in authority before the meeting to give them a heads up about issues or topics and also to check in on where they stand.

During the meeting, try to treat them like other participants, except at moments when it makes sense to explicitly acknowledge their authority. For example, if you look at the superintendent before you make a comment or after you ask a question, it might appear that you're seeking approval or that her response should be first. However, when the authority is relevant, name it; for example, "Superintendent Holmes will be the final decision maker on this, but I know she really wants to hear what we have to say about it." You might also check in with that person during a break or small group work to see how things are going from her perspective and to see if she has any advice about adjustments.

WHEN YOU HAVE MORE AUTHORITY THAN OTHERS This scenario can also be tricky because in a way you have double authority—from your position outside the meeting and your facilitator role within the meeting.

There are no easy guideposts and tactics here. You can try stepping out of the facilitator role explicitly if you do have information or an opinion to share. If you have an opinion, recognize that it will probably carry more weight in the conversation than most other people's opinions. Often, this means not sharing your opinion right away. However, if you always share your opinion at the end, sometimes people just wait for it or don't think that what comes before matters. To counter this impression, try sharing your opinion early and make clear that you want to hear other opinions, particularly challenges and disagreements with it. Or, when you share later, include what you had been thinking as well as how your thinking is evolving based on the conversation in the meeting.

✳ ✳ ✳

Wise facilitation can be developed over time by mindfully keeping to (and deviating from) the agenda, supporting full engagement, managing conflict, and maintaining awareness of the role you play. Thoughtfully addressing dilemmas as they occur, ideally with the support of a colleague, also helps.

Try It Yourself
Test-Drive Facilitation Tips

As a facilitator, you're trying to keep the purpose in mind, be focused yet flexible, be intentional (including about choosing not to do something), and enlist help when you need it. Whew! That's a lot. Now it's time to try it.

1. Pick two of the top tips for facilitators that you would like to follow when you facilitate the meeting you planned at the end of chapter 3.

2. Test out those tips as you facilitate the meeting.

3. Reflect independently on what you noticed as you used the agenda and tried to follow the tips.

4. Think back to the foundational and recurring setup tasks you did in advance of the meeting. Which of them contributed to meeting effectiveness? Which turned out to be less important than you expected?

5. Have a conversation with your meeting buddy about how the meeting went and what you learned about agenda making and facilitating.

6. Review the common dilemmas for facilitators. Did you encounter these or other dilemmas? Reflect on how you handled them or how you might address them differently in the future.

7. Write down one thing you want to keep doing and one thing you want to improve the next time you facilitate a meeting.

6

WISE PARTICIPATION

IN GREAT MEETINGS, it's not just the facilitators who are at the top of their game; participants bring their full selves to the experience as well. So for this chapter, put on your participant hat. As you think deeply about what's involved in this role, don't be surprised if some of your insights about how to be an effective participant inform the way you think about facilitation too.

The word "participate" comes from the Latin words "pars" (part) and "capere" (to take). At the simplest level, the job of the participant is to take part in the meeting. Note that "participate" does not come from words meaning "to take all of" or "to take none of." Participants have a critical part to play, and it is important for everyone to appreciate that participants' job is to work with the facilitator and one another to make the meeting successful.

Participants can do many things the facilitator can do, so many of the top tips in Exhibit 5.1 can apply to both roles. *But participants can also do some things the facilitator can't.* For example, as a participant, it may be easier for you to challenge a point than it is for the facilitator, who may need to remain more neutral. It can also be easier for you to name an elephant in the room, or to support or nudge colleagues who are not engaging as productively they could be.

In this chapter, we describe top tips (see Exhibit 6.1) as well as common dilemmas (see Exhibit 6.2) for each of the tasks that we introduced in chapter 5: keeping to (and deviating from) the agenda, supporting full engagement, managing conflict, and maintaining awareness of the role you play.

Exhibit 6.1

Top Tips for Participants	
TASK	**TOP TIPS**
1 Keeping to (and Deviating from) the Agenda	• Be on time • Understand the purpose
2 Supporting Full Engagement	• Think before you sit • Follow norms • Use people's names • Be fully present • Build on the ideas of others
3 Managing Conflict	• Be courageous • Challenge ideas, not people
4 Maintaining Awareness of the Role You Play	• Be mindful of preferences • Weigh your words • Provide constructive feedback

Exhibit 6.2

Common Dilemmas for Participants	
TASK	**DILEMMA**
1 Keeping to (and Deviating from) the Agenda	• You think the meeting is serving the wrong purpose • There's an elephant in the room
2 Supporting Full Engagement	• You're unprepared • You're talking too much • You're talking too little • You're participating virtually
3 Managing Conflict	• Everyone is playing nice • Someone else is upset • You're upset • You want to help the facilitator • You want to challenge the facilitator
4 Maintaining Awareness of the Role You Play	• You have significant positional authority • You're more comfortable facilitating than participating

TASK 1: KEEPING TO (AND DEVIATING FROM) THE AGENDA

One of the arenas in which participants have the most influence is how well the meeting sticks to the agenda. Participants can help a meeting stay on track, derail it entirely, or identify when a detour may be just the thing the meeting needs to make progress. It is not the participants' role (or even the facilitator's role) to make sure the meeting sticks to the agenda exactly as written. As discussed in chapter 5, there are times when it makes a lot of sense to adjust the agenda in the moment. But sometimes it's easier for *participants* to see when an adjustment is needed than it is for the facilitator, who may be invested in the agenda and absorbed by meeting dynamics. As a participant, you need to be thinking about both how you can help the meeting stay on track and how to intervene when you believe the group would be better off switching tracks.

Top Tips

BE ON TIME There is little hope that a meeting will stick to the agenda if participants wander in at their own convenience. If you know in advance that you have a prior commitment that will make it impossible for you to be on time, let the facilitator know ahead of time. That way, the facilitator can explain that you are on your way as the meeting is called to order. This courtesy applies not just to actual time conflicts on your calendar but also to hidden conflicts. We have never once been able to walk out of one room at 10:00 a.m. and then instantaneously arrive in another building for a 10:00 a.m. start to a different meeting (though we like to imagine we can when we commit to both meetings!).

UNDERSTAND THE PURPOSE Make sure you understand the purpose of the meeting. If you don't, ask— chances are you are not the only one. But be aware that the way you phrase the question can signal either that you're trying to *understand* or *challenge* the purpose. For example, if you ask, "Why are we having this meeting?" it might sound to some ears like you believe it's not worth having the meeting or that you don't agree with the reasoning, whereas "I'm not entirely clear on our purpose here. I want to be able to help us have a great meeting, so could we clarify what we are trying to accomplish?" makes it clear that you're asking for your own benefit, not to challenge the decision to meet in the first place. Also, by saying "we," you are signaling that you're part of the "we" that is committed to having a productive session.

Knowing the purpose will make it easier for you to know the kinds of comments that will be most valuable to the group and will also help you decide whether you want to speak up in favor of adjusting the agenda. For example, you could say, "I know we are trying to develop a shared understanding of what the teacher evaluation system looks like, but right now it feels like we agree on the individual components but not how they connect to one another. Could we add some time to the agenda so we can literally sketch a map that puts all these pieces together? If we move on without doing that, I'm concerned that we'll be building on a shaky foundation."

Common Dilemmas

WHEN YOU THINK THE MEETING IS SERVING THE WRONG PURPOSE If the facilitator used the Meeting Wise Checklist when planning the agenda, the purpose of the meeting is clearly stated. If, as a participant, you followed our top tip to "understand the purpose," you made sure to get crystal clear on what the meeting is about. But what if you think it should be about *something else*?

The ideal time to raise this, of course, is when the facilitator sends the agenda out for comment before the meeting. But if you do not get the agenda ahead of time, or if during the meeting you get a sudden flash of insight, you can speak up. In fact, in our experience, participants are quite frequently the ones who figure out that the objectives are wrong and the meeting needs redirection. This can sound like, "Are we sure these are the most essential things to be spending our limited time on today? I'm wondering if X would make more sense given [new context or information, level of preparation of the group, etc.]." This approach offers both an alternative and an explanation for why it might make sense to shift. Or, "I appreciate this thoughtful agenda and the conversation we're having, but I have to admit I'm feeling a lot of urgency around Y. Am I the only one?" This makes clear where you are coming from and shows your appreciation of the need to get multiple perspectives on your hunch.

If you decide to question the purpose, the key is to do that in the spirit of moving this group, *not your personal agenda*, forward. When your own agenda is making it hard for you to participate in the meeting, sometimes it helps to just name it so that you can move on. For example, "I know this isn't what we're meeting about today, but I'd like to put Z in a parking lot for future discussion so that I can get the issue out there and focus on what we are doing today." Again, it's ideal to raise this before the meeting starts, but better late than never if it helps you attend to the agenda at hand.

WHEN THERE'S AN ELEPHANT IN THE ROOM Nobody's talking about them, but they're called "elephants" because they are so big that everyone is aware of them—every minute. Maybe nobody wants to discuss these large, looming issues; or maybe some people want to discuss them, but there's a fear of what will happen. Deep down, as a participant you may feel that unless you *do* discuss them, your group might be unable to do authentic work.

You could discuss your concern with the facilitator before the meeting takes place. But sometimes the elephant rears its bulk right there in the meeting. What then? You can start by bringing the elephant into plain sight: "I'm feeling like there's an elephant in the room that we're avoiding. It seems like we're scared to say the word 'race,' much less talk about it. Does anyone else get that sense?" or "We seem to be dancing around the issue here, which I would say is some of us not following through on what we said we'd do." Just by naming it, you've introduced the problem explicitly. This approach also allows others the opportunity to offer a different version of the elephant or to think about how to engage it.

Once the elephant is named, test the waters on whether this is the right time to talk about it. Discussing elephants almost by definition takes the agenda off track, but it also has the potential of serving the group's long-term purpose by allowing people to address something that is holding the group back. The questions the group faces are whether to engage the topic now and if so, how, and if not, when to and how to make progress in the interim. As a participant, you can point out the options in a way that shows the facilitator you are not out to hijack the meeting, "This seems important. What do people think about talking about this right now?" or "This seems critical, and yet we need to make some decisions here. Do we feel like it's a good use of our time right now to discuss this? And if not, can we commit to talking about it at a future meeting?"

TASK 2: SUPPORTING FULL ENGAGEMENT

There are many ways to participate: listening, thinking, talking, asking questions. Just because a participant is quiet doesn't mean he isn't fully engaged, and just because someone is making lots of comments doesn't mean she is fully present. When you are a participant, supporting full engagement begins with managing yourself and extends to helping others engage productively.

Top Tips

THINK BEFORE YOU SIT Watch where you sit, and whom you sit next to, since this could affect both yours and others' ability to participate. Sitting next to a friend can be distracting if it tempts you to have side conversations. But it can be a very good idea if it gives you more confidence to participate fully or if it helps you manage that person toward being a more effective participant.

If you have a choice about where you sit, try sitting in a new seat once in a while. When we mix things up, we find it almost always offers a new perspective on the conversation, and it can sometimes shift the group's participation dynamics in a positive way.

FOLLOW NORMS The Golden Rule applies here as in other aspects of life: do unto others as you would have them do unto you (or, as we like to say, "be the meeting participant you want to interact with"). As we mentioned in chapter 1, this book assumes that your group has set norms (see chapter 4 for a description of what this involves). For those norms to have any power, each individual needs to take responsibility for knowing what the norms are and for following them. If you're in a meeting without explicit norms, be guided by general laws of civility—take turns, don't interrupt, and be polite. If you think the group would benefit from an explicit conversation about norms, suggest it.

USE PEOPLE'S NAMES A small but important point is to know and use people's names whenever possible. Using names is respectful and helps people know you see and hear them. If there are no nametags and you don't know everyone's name, introduce yourself, or ask for introductions. We often make ourselves a little map with names matched with seating positions so that we can refer to people by name throughout the conversation.

BE FULLY PRESENT When you're in a meeting, be there 100 percent. There are no doubt plenty of other things you could be doing with the time, some of which may feel more urgent or appealing. But if the meeting's purpose is worthy, give it your full attention. You, your fellow meeting participants, the facilitator, *and the children whose education depends on you* deserve that.

Two things can help you be fully present. The first is to make a deliberate transition into the meeting. Try to let go of whatever was happening or on your mind right before the meeting. Arriving a few minutes early, reviewing the agenda, and chatting with other colleagues can help you be ready and relaxed for the session at hand. And if you're arriving just in the nick of time, take a deep breath, remind yourself why you are there, and dive in.

The second thing participants can do is to eliminate distractions. Just because it is now technologically possible to answer e-mail, check weather, and order socks from a handheld device beneath the table *doesn't mean it's a good idea.* Neuroscientists have assembled solid evidence that the human brain cannot actually do two things at once. Sure, a person can hear what's happening in the background as she rearranges her electronic calendar, but the plain fact is that no one can give full attention to a meeting and solving a scheduling puzzle at the same time.

Eliminating distractions also avoids the plain rudeness of being off task. Yes, we know that multitasking during meetings is becoming normal in some organizations. But back to the Golden Rule—how do *you* feel if you're talking and someone is e-mailing or working on something else? For us, this signals, "I have something to do that's more important than listening to you"—not the best spirit in which to have a collaborative, learning-oriented meeting. (If this is a particular issue in your setting, you may want to recommend adding "Be here now" or the more direct "No checking e-mail or texts" to your list of group norms.)

BUILD ON THE IDEAS OF OTHERS There are times in some meetings when people are tripping over one another to get their ideas out. In this situation, it can be particularly helpful if participants commit to building on others' ideas, or what Pixar calls "plussing." Pixar relies heavily on ideas, creativity, and collaboration to make its highly successful animated movies. Former dean of Pixar University Randy Nelson describes

Pixar's "plussing" approach as relying on two principles from improvisation: "Accept every offer" and "Make your partner look good."[1] Basically, whatever someone says, don't judge it but instead try to build on it. This is different than inquiry, in which you try to understand the idea. In "plussing," you run with whatever is on the table and see where it takes you. It's an "and" approach instead of a "but" approach. Try that in a meeting—even or especially with something you disagree with—and see what happens.

Common Dilemmas

WHEN YOU'RE UNPREPARED Even if the facilitator doesn't ask about preparation directly, it is participants' responsibility to come clean right away if they are not ready to participate fully. This can sound like "I've reviewed the agenda carefully, but wasn't able to read the article" or "I know I promised to get estimates from vendors for this meeting, but I won't be able to do that until later this week."

Saying something up front helps participants avoid spending energy trying to cover up or manage any guilt or embarrassment about not being prepared. Our experience as participants is that the longer we wait, the harder it is to confess, both because we've now protected the information for a while and because the "right" time to slip it in never seems to come about. We like to think our transparency helps the facilitator know where things stand and consider any adjustments that might be needed. When possible, we communicate our preparation to the group instead of opting for a private conversation with the facilitator. This often makes it easier for others to admit their lapses too.

No matter your level of preparation, look for a way to contribute anyway. Can you listen carefully and reflect back what you're hearing? Can you ask questions to deepen understanding of someone else's point? Is there a more formal role you might take on, like process checker or note taker?

WHEN YOU'RE TALKING TOO MUCH A big part of your job as a participant is to manage your own airtime. If you know you're a big talker, remember this: it's easier for *you* to manage yourself than it is for other people to try to reign you in. There are several strategies you can try. One is to simply tally how many times you talk compared with other people. Seeing your own data may be all you need to appreciate the need for forbearance; the very act of collecting the data might even cause you to change your behavior in the moment.

A related idea is to use a physical reminder every time you speak. In chapter 5, we recommend that facilitators use tokens or a talking stick to help regulate participation. Even if the group isn't using such a technique, you could have some sort of "chips" for yourself. If this feels odd to you, try to go for the humorous angle by making your strategy public. If you think you talk too much, chances are you're not the only one in the group who shares that opinion! Your colleagues will likely welcome and support your use of stones or quarters or whatever you have on hand. And using tokens of some kind may give you pause and help you decide whether what you have to say is worth using up a token.

If all this feels too complicated, a simple resolution to hear a certain number of other voices before you talk again can also be effective. Our favorite number for this technique is three, as in wait "three before me," but you can use your judgment what number makes the most sense for a particular meeting.

Not all strategies require counting. You can write down your thoughts instead of speaking them out loud. This will help you remember them to share later, or will give them an outlet other than your mouth. Or you can enlist a buddy to help. If you know you tend to go on too long or pipe up too frequently but find it hard to monitor yourself, have someone help you know in the moment when you're doing it. Your buddy might sit next to you and give you a little elbow or nudge. Or he or she could sit across from you and give you certain look or other signal you've worked out in advance. You can also ask for feedback *after* the meeting, and your colleagues will be most helpful if you tell them *before* the meeting what you want them to keep think about: "I'm really trying to work on managing my airtime. Would you be willing after the meeting to let me know whether I seemed to be talking too much, not enough, or just right? And could you help me think about which of my contributions are most helpful?"

WHEN YOU'RE TALKING TOO LITTLE Though thinking and listening are important modes of participating, managing your own airtime does include making sure you also participate out loud. Otherwise, the group is missing the opportunity to learn from you. Between us, Liz tends to fall on the "talking too much" end of the continuum while Kathy tends to fall on the "talking too little" side. Liz can say with certainty that Kathy and others who fall on this end often have the most insightful and helpful things to contribute—mostly because they've been doing more listening and thinking than those of us who are talkers.

Sparse talkers can use some of the same strategies as the big talkers, but with a twist. The simplest may be to just set a goal. It might be as general as "Talk more this meeting," or, as with many goals, it might be easier if you set a concrete number, like "Talk twice today."

Another way is to try and speak early in the meeting. While this approach is usually counterintuitive for people who prefer to listen for a while before speaking, it works well if you remember that your contribution doesn't have to be *profound* to be *helpful*. Kathy found this advice particularly useful, since she used to set a high bar for how meaningful or valuable or well developed a thought needed to be before she would say it out loud. In the meantime, she saw that lots of other people were saying somewhat ordinary things that helped move the meeting along. Before she knew it, she'd be feeling self-conscious that she hadn't weighed in yet. This led her to believe that when she did speak, she should have something *really* brilliant to say, which of course raised the bar even higher and made her hold back even more.

Remember, as a participant, you are not solely responsible for a thoughtful meeting. You're taking part, and your part is to contribute something, even if not fully formed. If you're not ready to make a statement, ask a question. The longer you wait to contribute, the less influential your comment might be because the rest of the group won't have as much time to build on it and work with it.

An alternative strategy is to write down your thoughts. While this approach encourages a big talker to slow down her thinking, it can also help a quieter person solidify his ideas and feel more prepared to share.

Finally, you can always ask for feedback from someone at the meeting. Just as with big talkers, asking for a buddy's take on the frequency and usefulness of your contributions can be illuminating. And you can talk with the facilitator between meetings to ask for help that will support you in participating more. For example, as facilitators, we've had participants say things to us like, "I'm having a hard time jumping in because by the time I've formulated my thought, the conversation has moved on to another topic. Could you sometimes give us a chance to write or think before speaking?"

WHEN YOU'RE PARTICIPATING VIRTUALLY When you are participating in a meeting via phone or videoconference, it can be particularly challenging to engage fully and to make space for others to participate.

Our top tip to "be fully present" is especially important—and challenging—in this situation. It is all the more tempting to check your e-mail and multitask when no one else can see you doing it. But remember, you can't do two things well at the same time. Do the meeting. For most of us, this means shutting down e-mail and other temptations entirely.

If there are multiple people participating virtually, say your name when you jump in so that everyone can keep track of who's talking: "This is Penelope. I recommend that we . . ." And when you're not talking, keep the sound muted on your end to help limit background noise. You could also volunteer for a role, like note taker or timekeeper, if you think that will help you focus. Even if you don't have a formal role, take some kind of notes for yourself while the conversation is happening to help you pay attention.

And finally, if you are participating with audio only, take advantage of the fact that you can walk or change positions as often as you like. As we mentioned earlier, movement helps your brain work better.

TASK 3: MANAGING CONFLICT

When you hear the word "conflict," does your pulse quicken with anticipation of something exciting, or with dread of something dangerous? People have different comfort levels with conflict, and many education cultures are quite protective and "nice," making the existence of conflict seem like evidence that something is wrong. As discussed in chapter 5, conflict can be very helpful in meetings—productive meetings often have both heat and light. As a participant, you can help generate both and help the group manage discomfort in ways that often facilitators cannot do.

Top Tips

BE COURAGEOUS Your vulnerability opens doors for others. When you're courageous and dive into a place that feels scary or uncomfortable, you not only bring important ideas and perspectives into the meeting, you also help others be more courageous. This is particularly true when you focus on your own experience and emotions, not on others'. You may have heard elsewhere that people are more receptive to statements that begin with "I" than those that make blanket judgments. We find this is absolutely true in meetings. "I'm feeling anxious about this decision" can open the door to a more productive conversation than "This decision is irresponsible," just as "I'm confused" is almost always more effective than "You're not making any sense." Some people find it helpful to make their discomfort public as a way of signaling to others that they're outside their comfort zone: "I'm going to take a risk right now and say . . ." "Though it makes me uncomfortable, I feel I have to share . . ."

CHALLENGE IDEAS, NOT PEOPLE Sometimes it takes courage to challenge something you disagree with, and sometimes it doesn't, but in either case, separate people and ideas. A subtle change in language can makes the challenge feel less personal, which makes it safer for everyone to engage. For example, instead of "Diana, you don't have a bold enough vision for what this organization could be," try "Let's look closely at the vision for this organization. Could we make it more ambitious?" This framing can make a large difference in the tone, safety, and focus of the discussion.

Incidentally, focusing on ideas, not people, is just as wise of a practice when you are agreeing with something as when you are challenging it. Instead of "Diana, you solved our problem," focus more on the idea and then build on it: "What if we took Diana's idea and did it with students, not just teachers?" You may also find it helpful to preface your comment by calling attention to the presence of a difference of opinion. We find that starting a challenge with "I'd like to push back on that" keeps the focus on the "that" and not on the person who said it.

Common Dilemmas

WHEN EVERYONE IS PLAYING NICE Sometimes there is not enough heat or light in a discussion. Maybe everyone is agreeing with each other, and there is no glimmer of dissension or another perspective. As a participant, one of the easiest ways to shake things up is to play devil's advocate. Try on an opinion you don't necessarily believe—not to waste time but to help the group think out of the box. For example, "I'm going to play devil's advocate here and argue that we shouldn't be in the business of addressing X." Or you can try on the potential point of view of someone who's not in the room: "I'm trying to think about what this might feel like from a parent's perspective. If I were a parent, I think I'd be a lot more worried about Y than about . . ." You can also propose counterarguments, point out gaps in logic, and invite others to do the same: "This makes a lot of sense to me, but I'm trying to think about what we might be missing. Where are the places our ideas might fall apart? It looks like we might be a little too optimistic about Z. In the past, things have never gone that smoothly. What can we learn from past experience?"

WHEN SOMEONE ELSE IS UPSET When someone is upset in the meeting, trying to make the person feel better right then and there usually makes it worse. Most people need some time away from the spotlight to get emotions under control, so having more attention at that moment can be counterproductive. And besides, people who are upset may not *want* to feel better in that moment. Do, however, check in with them during a break or after the meeting, ask how they're doing, and be a listener. If they don't want to talk about it, respect that.

Try not to take someone else's anxiety on as your own. If someone is anxious about something and you're anxious about that person being anxious, you're less able to help the meeting move forward productively, whether that's attending directly to an issue or moving on to something else.

And finally, you can help the facilitator contain the heat so that it doesn't become a raging fire—but try to not extinguish it entirely. Remember, heat can be helpful even if some people are upset or uncomfortable. Like the facilitator, you can acknowledge emotions and reactions and also encourage the group to stay close to the heat for a little while: "I'm seeing a range of reactions to this topic, and even though it might be really uncomfortable, I'm hoping we can stay with this for a little while because I think it will help us move forward."

WHEN YOU'RE UPSET It's even harder when the upset person is *you*! First, be attuned to your own signs that you're upset. When those signals go off, whether they're apparent to others or only to you, proceed with caution and give yourself a little time and space if you can. Be careful of what you say when upset, which doesn't mean be silent, but do recognize that it's harder to do things like make "I" statements, separate people and ideas, and treat others the way you want to be treated when your emotions are running high. Try taking a time-out, whether that's by not speaking right away or breathing intentionally or drinking some water or getting up to replenish your snack plate. Look at someone you trust in the room. And if someone is pushing or inviting you to speak and you're not sure what will come out of your mouth (or you're sure, and it's not going to be productive), ask for some time, like: "Thanks for the question. I think I'm going to listen for a little while before I respond."

In addition to those behaviors, we find helpful something that a colleague once passed along: the things that drive you the craziest may be the ones you fear most in yourself. So when we're really upset with someone, we try to remember that our response may be telling us at least as much about ourselves as it is about someone else. This little reminder gives us enough pause to exhale and direct some of our emotion at self-inquiry.

WHEN YOU WANT TO HELP THE FACILITATOR In heated moments, the facilitator has a tough job. And if he is floundering or seems to be missing important cues, your inclination might be to come to the rescue. However, the most tactful and helpful moves we've seen (and experienced gratefully) focus not on the facilitator, but on moving the *group* forward. For example, instead of "George, I think you're missing something here" or "George, this meeting is getting out of hand," how about something like "We seem to be missing something here, and that's about X" or "What if we all took a minute to think about how this suggestion does or doesn't match with our own experience and evidence, and then share out?"

Both of the revised suggestions explicitly take the facilitator out of the mix and instead focus on the group and "we." The second also offers a suggestion for what to do, which can be very helpful to the facilitator, who might be too flustered to see a path out of the weeds. Another way to help the facilitator more directly is privately, one-on-one, during a break or group work, when you can offer your perspective on what's happening and why and suggestions for what to do. This approach will leave the facilitator room to take up your suggestion or not without having to make that decision in front of others.

WHEN YOU WANT TO CHALLENGE THE FACILITATOR Perhaps you disagree with the facilitator, either with a choice she has made or with something she has said. This is a different situation than trying to help a facilitator get unstuck or pointing out something the facilitator may have missed, which are usually ways of supporting the facilitator. Although a challenge might ultimately support the facilitator and the meeting, it matters a lot how you do it. Done carefully and respectfully, the challenge can help make the meeting a place where multiple voices are heard and honored, and the facilitator can be very grateful for the help. Done not so respectfully or carefully, the challenge can undermine the facilitator's role, either in her own eyes, the group's, or both.

Before challenging the facilitator, first ask yourself, "How will this help the meeting objectives? Is this about my own agenda, or will this help move the meeting forward?" If you persuade yourself that your intervention will help the group, offer your perspective and if possible, a way to proceed that leaves the facilitator room to opt in or out. For example, "Stacy, I didn't hear that the same way you did. What I heard Zula say was _____. Zula, could you explain that to us again?" This approach puts the focus on Zula and allows the possibility that you, too, could have misunderstood.

TASK 4: MAINTAINING AWARENESS OF THE ROLE YOU PLAY

A common theme of this chapter has been that participants need to self-regulate and be aware of the ways in which they are—or are not—helping the group to meet its objectives. In chapter 1, we discussed the importance of having everyone in the educational sector understand how the meetings they attend connect to the ultimate goal of helping all children learn. If participants require the facilitator or other participants to spend precious time or energy helping them take part productively in the meeting, or if participants are dutifully attending meetings but not rising to the occasion and tackling hard problems, there's less time and energy going toward that very important purpose. So keep in mind: in your role as a participant, you have the power to make it much easier or much, much harder for a meeting to make a meaningful contribution to learning.

Top Tips

BE MINDFUL OF PREFERENCES One thing you can do to develop awareness of your role is to reflect on your natural inclinations when working with others. In chapter 4, we describe some strategies for getting preferences out in the open.

As a participant, your job is to appreciate that everyone has preferences about interacting with others and making sense of the world. Sometimes they're strong across-the-board preferences, and sometimes they can vary by context. These preferences aren't inherently good or bad, but they do affect how you and others participate in meetings. When you are aware of preferences, you can tap into them when they'll help move the meeting forward or check them when they are getting in the way of the meeting. You may also be able to see when you might need to step out of your preferred way of acting to help move the meeting forward.

It's also helpful to remember that other people in the meeting have different preferences from yours. This can be easy to know intellectually but hard to remember in the moment.

As a participant, you can actively think about your own preferences and how those might help or hinder the current meeting, and adjust accordingly. You can also make your preferences known and make requests that will help you. For example, you might say, "I need a little more processing time. Could we take a couple of minutes to just think about the proposal on the table before we discuss it?" or "I need to understand the big picture before I can dive into details. Can we talk about the 'why' here?" or "This conversation is a little too abstract for me. Can someone give me a picture of what it would look like on the ground?" You know best what you need, so as a participant it is important for you to ask for it.

WEIGH YOUR WORDS At the most basic level, your roles as a participant are to listen and contribute. When you want to make a comment on something about which you feel strongly, it is important to do so in a way that other participants can hear it. It is also important to make sure you take the time to fully understand the position of others. Robert Garmston and Bruce Wellman point out the value of striking a balance between advocacy and inquiry.[2] Inquiry involves working to better understand *other people's* perspectives, and advocacy involves trying to help people better understand *your* perspective (although occasionally you may play "devil's advocate" and speak on behalf of a position you don't feel strongly about yourself but think would be valuable for the group to consider).

Advocacy can help others see a fresh perspective, save the group from a bad decision, or motivate the group to action. But it matters *how* you share that perspective. In *Learning by Doing*, DuFour et al. recommend that when advocating, you not only give your opinion but also:

- State your assumptions

- Describe your reasoning

- Give concrete examples

- Reveal your perspective

- Acknowledge other perspectives.[3]

After advocating, you can actively invite others to help consider the position by saying things like, "Clearly, I feel really strongly about this, but I'm guessing other people might feel strongly in a different direction or you might be able to see things that I'm missing here. What questions do you have?" or even more encouraging, "I feel so strongly about this that it's hard for me to see other perspectives. Can you help me by sharing an alternative perspective or challenging some of my assumptions?" After advocating, we like to wait until at least two other people have spoken before speaking again. That provides some space for listening.

When someone else voices a strong opinion, you have an opportunity to respond by taking an inquiry stance, which might sound like:

- What led you to that conclusion?

- Can you help me understand your thinking here?

- Which aspects of what you have proposed do you feel are most significant or essential?

- I'm hearing your primary goal is . . .[4]

Be careful, though, of questions that are really about poking holes in someone else's argument to bolster a different perspective (that's advocacy) versus questions that are about better understanding the perspective on the table (that's inquiry).

PROVIDE CONSTRUCTIVE FEEDBACK Feedback has been a consistent theme throughout this book. The Meeting Wise Checklist encourages incorporation of feedback into agenda design, as well as reflection time at the end of every meeting for collecting that feedback. And guess who's doing most of the reflecting? You and your fellow participants! The feedback will only be as thoughtful as you collectively make it. So when offered the opportunity, be sure to let the group know what worked well about the collaborative experience, what you think needs to be improved, and how to improve it.

If the facilitator does not give you a formal opportunity to provide real feedback, you can still contribute your reflections. When something worked really well in the meeting, your warm feedback will find willing ears. But what if you see lots of room for improvement? In that case, you have to decide if it is worth your time to find a way to make things better. How likely is it that your feedback will be taken seriously and in the right spirit? Will you somehow be "punished" by speaking up (perhaps even by being tasked with having to fix everything yourself)? You may decide that providing unsolicited feedback is a bad idea. That's OK. We do that, too. That means sometimes we settle for meetings that we know are not as great as they could be.

However, we only let ourselves off the hook for giving feedback if the meeting itself is not essential to the work we do. So if you believe a meeting is (or should be) essential to your core work (for example, regular teacher team meetings, principal meetings, leadership team meetings, meetings with your close colleagues), *challenge yourself to figure out how to share your ideas for improvement.* Maybe you provide feedback privately. Maybe you get people together and offer a suggestion from the group. Who knows, maybe you suggest that everyone evaluate the next meeting's agenda against the Meeting Wise Checklist! The thing to remember is that if participants tolerate bad meetings, the price paid is high. Kids lose.

And by the way: debriefing the meeting with a colleague who has no role in designing the next agenda or facilitating the meeting doesn't count as "feedback." That kind of conversation is usually more like complaining or venting or processing. When you think about it, how many gripe sessions out in a parking lot actually translate into constructive suggestions that lead to better meetings?

Common Dilemmas

WHEN YOU HAVE SIGNIFICANT POSITIONAL AUTHORITY When you have the most or significant positional authority in the room (for example, you're the principal in a room full of teachers or the superintendent in a room full of principals, teachers, and administrators), your role as a participant can be tricky. The key is being aware of the fact that what you do or say has the power to sway the direction of the meeting and potentially undermine the facilitator's ability to do his or her job. Sometimes this is less about what you do and more about what you represent and how other people in the room relate to your position. Regardless, there are some things you can do (and not do) to encourage others to fully participate.

First, choose carefully where you sit. Try not to sit at the head of the table, which would reinforce your authority. Also, avoid speaking first, since your comments are likely to influence the conversation in a particular direction. In deciding when to speak, take care not to become the focus of the discussion. When you do speak, trend toward inquiry over advocacy when you can. This will help both you and your fellow participants really unpack the issues on the table. You can of course advocate for a position, but when you do so, avoid outright praise or critique of ideas. "That's a terrific suggestion, Pat!" is a less useful statement to the group than "Your suggestion to involve students in the decision making process makes sense to me because we need their involvement if this pilot is going to succeed." Remember, your opinion may carry more weight than you realize.

Finally, when you are listening, be intentional when you make eye contact. The same strategies about eye contact that apply to facilitators apply to people with significant authority. Eyes and comments will tend to go toward you, so if you want to encourage people to talk to each other and not to look to you for approval, try looking down at your papers, or reaching into your bag for something, or looking around the room. This will encourage the speaker to find another visual target for her or his comment.

WHEN YOU'RE MORE COMFORTABLE FACILITATING THAN PARTICIPATING If you spend most of your time in meetings facilitating and don't get much time participating, you may find that you'd rather drive the bus than be a passenger. And you may be a bit of a backseat driver at that—inwardly critiquing the way the meeting is being run and thinking of all the ways you could be doing better. If this rings true for you, you have two options. One is to challenge yourself to observe the meeting as dispassionately as you can, and then use either the Meeting Wise Checklist or the Top Tips for Facilitators to help you identify a couple of very specific recommendations for next time. Maybe the facilitator needs to be taking on fewer roles. Maybe a discussion protocol would help get more people engaged. Maybe the group needs to revisit its purpose. Allow your considerable facilitation experience to be an asset to the group—one that supports, not undermines the facilitator's growth.

Your other option is to look inward. You can do this by reviewing the Top Tips for Participants and considering whether *you* are doing everything you can to make the meeting successful. Kathy was feeling a bit holier-than-thou about a series of meetings a few years ago, and found herself jumping to the conclusion that the facilitator was the problem. But when she decided to look hard at her own participation, she realized that she was sitting back and just letting the meeting happen, doing nothing to steer the group away from continually grazing the same old ground. So she resolved to participate more constructively, proposing that the group commit to a much more ambitious goal than they ever had. She was heartened to see that, far from feeling threatened by her idea, the facilitator seemed relieved and even energized by the suggestion. Turns out, the facilitator was never really the problem—she just needed participants to meet her halfway.

Being a participant in a meeting is a little like being part of a team performance. Kathy used to sing in an *a cappella* group, and Liz used to play basketball. In both cases, the talents each team member brought mattered a lot, as did the choices they made while the game or concert was under way. But it also mattered how they played with everyone else. Even the most skillful shooters and singers couldn't be successful on their own. They had to figure out how to make their colleagues better, too, in order for the group to be successful.

✳ ✳ ✳

As a participant, sometimes it can feel like a lot of the meeting isn't in your control. Maybe you didn't set the agenda. Maybe you'd rather be facilitating. Maybe other participants aren't observing the Golden Rule. Maybe the meeting isn't as "meeting wise" as you'd like it to be. No matter the situation, you still have a role to play, and the wiser your participation, the more influence you can have.

Try It Yourself
Test-Drive Participation Tips

Give yourself the freedom to explore the participants' role in new ways.

1. Pick two or three of the Top Tips for Participants that you would like to try.

2. Test out those tips as you participate in a meeting.

3. Reflect independently on what you noticed as you tried to follow the tips.

4. Discuss the experience with your meeting buddy. What happened? What insights did you have that would help you become a better participant? What insights would you apply to being an agenda maker and meeting facilitator?

5. Review the Common Dilemmas for Participants in this chapter. Did you encounter these or other dilemmas? Discuss how you handled them or how you might address them differently in the future.

6. Write down one thing you want to keep doing and one thing you want to improve the next time you participate in a meeting.

7

BECOMING MEETING WISE

IMPROVING THE QUALITY OF meetings, like improving anything, is a process. You play an important role in this process, so do your individual part, working on what you have direct control over, such as your own facilitation and participation. But that won't be enough, because meetings are *collaborative* efforts—if you could single-handedly achieve the meeting purpose, you wouldn't need a meeting in the first place! At some point, you need to involve your colleagues in making the most of collaborative time. And while a small group of colleagues can make their meetings soar, imagine what would happen if the whole organization were having purposeful, learning-centered meetings that engaged and challenged all participants!

We're not claiming that this is easy work. Or quick work. Or even that everyone will embrace it with open arms. Surrendering work habits, unproductive as they may be, can feel like a loss. Learning to have effective meetings, like all learning, includes experimentation and mistakes and takes time. But it can be done.

You may think that a radical shift is just what is needed to shake things up and make a clean break with business as usual, or you may feel that smaller steps could be more effective. The bigger the change and the fewer people proposing it, the more we encourage you to "go slow to go fast." The group needs to develop capacity to have wise meetings over time. Thus, our recommendation is to engage your colleagues as much as possible in naming that a shift that is needed and figuring out how to make it happen. Learning has a lot to do with motivation—this is as true for adults as for children—and being part of a change is much more motivating for most people than having it happen to them. Learning also has to do with a feeling of safety and challenge. Create a safe space for people to provide feedback—and within that safety, challenge the group to improve.

All that said, knowing how much to involve others will depend in part on the nature of the group that attends the meeting. If participants consider themselves part of an official team, such the "RHS Science Department," the "Beechwood City School Committee," or the "Bilingual Education Task Force," then dig in and plot the course together. However, if meeting participants have an informal (or perhaps even coincidental) connection to one another, as might be found at a statewide meeting of special education directors, a townwide meeting to welcome new families, or an athletic director's seasonal meeting for team coaches, you may make a different assessment. When people feel only loosely connected and do not perceive themselves as being charged with having to produce something collectively, you may find you are better off making some decisions yourself and then checking in to see how effectively meetings are helping the group achieve its stated goal.

If you and your colleagues truly believe that you can work together to improve the way you collaborate, you will not be stuck with the current quality level of your meetings. Figure out where you are now and accept that as the launch pad for improvement. *Wherever you are is where you are.* In most cases, you're not starting from scratch. Maybe you're midway through a series of meetings with a group that has met many times and has particular habits, some of which are not too productive. Even if you're starting fresh with a new group, that group may be embedded in an organizational culture that has habits and expectations. In either case, the question is, where do you start?

FINDING AN ENTRY POINT

We wrote this book to help you and your colleagues figure out what is happening (and not happening) today so that you can take actions to improve how you work together tomorrow. The way we see it, you have four entry points to becoming more meeting wise: making better agendas, investing in a firmer foundation, facilitating and participating more effectively, and tackling meeting dilemmas. Whichever door you decide to enter first, set a specific, small goal, try it out, and then check back on how well you've done against your goal.

Door #1: Make Better Agendas

If the problem is that your organization lacks a shared understanding of how to structure an effective meeting, the Meeting Wise Checklist might be just the place to start. Distribute the checklist and ask people to keep it in mind as they provide anonymous feedback about a meeting via index cards or an electronic survey. Or invite others to help you use the checklist to plan the next meeting (as several educators in the examples in chapter 3 did), and then solicit feedback from the whole group at the end of the next meeting.

Remember that all improvement is a journey. If you have lots of "no's" on the checklist, you're probably not going to be able to address all of them right away. Think about your meetings over time. What would you try in the next three meetings? What would your first move be? Ideally, pick an area that will make a dramatic difference in meeting quality. For example, if no one knows exactly why you are meeting, or if there is no pre-work, or if participants do a lot of listening and not much learning, addressing one of those issues could immediately help the group make good progress toward its goals. However, it could be that even smaller steps will help the group learn to behave differently. Try designating roles, allocating times to agenda items, building in time for feedback on the meeting, or writing down a few clear next steps from each meeting.

And if you are not used to even having an agenda, by all means start there. Choose a template (the Meeting Wise Agenda Template in the Quick Reference Guide is one option; you can modify it or create your own) and see what happens. If designed thoughtfully, the template can be a reminder to deal with most checklist items, like objectives, roles, time allocations, and assessment of the meeting.

Alternatively, the group could identify a subset of the checklist that everyone in your organization commits to working on, as described in "Try It *Yourselves*: Make a Collective Commitment to Creating Better Agendas."

Try It *Yourselves*
Make a Collective Commitment to Creating Better Agendas

1. Assemble a group of people from throughout your organization who have all read this book.

2. Have everyone take three to five quiet minutes to go through the Meeting Wise Checklist (see the Quick Reference Guide in the Resources section for a reproducible handout) and think about all the meetings they currently lead and attend. Ask them to put a star next to any questions that they wish they could answer "yes" to in all their meetings.

3. Write the key word from each of the 12 Meeting Wise Checklist questions on a piece of chart paper. Give each person up to five star stickers and have them place their stars on the chart near the questions they would like to see the organization as a whole commit to addressing.

4. Look at questions on the chart paper that have the most stars. Choose one to three questions that the group wants to collectively work on addressing better. Have a discussion that helps you come to a shared understanding of what meeting agendas would look like if they addressed these questions adequately.

5. Have everyone in the group commit to changing their practice so that they can authentically answer "yes" on this subset of questions when planning all their meetings in the coming month.

6. At the end of the month, reconvene the group to discuss what you learned. What happened? What should happen next?

Door #2: Invest in a Firmer Foundation

When you read chapter 4, you may have felt that you wanted to take on one or more of the foundational setup tasks—setting group norms, acknowledging work style preferences, developing an agenda template, and keeping track of your work—but that it didn't make sense for you to do those tasks on your own. Sometimes it's better to make investments *as an organization* so that you can build a shared culture around collaboration (the activity in "Try It *Yourselves*: Make a Collective Commitment to Investing in a Firmer Foundation" will get your team off to a good start). For example, Rose and Manuel of the Greenville School fifth-grade team example in chapter 3 might have wanted to have a better strategy for storing documents and capturing their learning. But having each grade-level team come up with its own electronic filing system would be inefficient at best. Working with the

Try It *Yourselves*
Make a Collective Commitment to Investing in a Firmer Foundation

1. Assemble a group of people from throughout your organization who have all read this book and done the "Try It Yourself" activity at the end of chapter 4.

2. Put four pieces of chart paper on the walls around the room, and write one of the foundational setup tasks from chapter 4 at the top of each paper: set group norms, acknowledge work style preferences, develop agenda template, keep track of your work.

3. Ask people to go to the chart paper that matches the foundational task that they identified as most important when they did the "Try It Yourself" activity at the end of chapter 4. Have people capture on the paper what they have done so far on this task and what they think the larger organization could do to support their efforts.

4. Have people rotate posters to see the ideas that their colleagues came up with and add their own thoughts.

5. Have an open discussion about insights generated and then commit to following through on something specific that the group believes will lay a firmer foundation for effective meetings.

6. Meet one month later to discuss the impact that doing the foundational task had on meeting quality. What happened? What should happen next?

school leadership team or the district to put a secure and easy document storage system in place would make a lot more sense.

Sometimes it's important to make an institutional decision to prioritize setting norms of interaction. In Jackson County, the superintendent and her deputy made time in their Monday morning leadership meetings for that particular group to set norms. But if norms were also an important missing piece throughout the system, providing a common norm-setting protocol, proposing a set of norms, and setting the expectation that norms should be followed could help the whole organization build a better foundation for its collaborative work.

If you feel a tension between developing high-functioning teams and getting stuff done, the key is to find a way to do both. Nothing builds trust and a sense of team as effectively as producing a high-quality shared product. For this reason, it is important to pair any deliberate work on an abstract concept such as "norms" or "work style preferences" with a real-world opportunity for people to create something valuable. For example, once norms are set, encouraging people throughout the system to focus on checklist question 2, "Have we chosen challenging activities that advance the meeting objectives and engage all participants?" will help ensure a return on your investment in group process.

Door #3: Improve Facilitation and Participation

What if you say "yes" to most things on the checklist and feel good about the foundation you have laid, but still believe that your organization could be using collaborative time better? In that case, focus on what happens *within* meetings. This is harder to control, since it depends on people's interactions. But precisely because what happens during meetings implicates everyone, focusing here can have a tremendous payoff.

Since so many things happen simultaneously in a meeting, breaking it down into manageable pieces can be helpful. Consider the four categories of actions that we offered in chapters 5 and 6: which might offer the most room for improvement? Is the group struggling with keeping to and deviating from the agenda, supporting full engagement, managing conflict, or with meeting members playing their roles effectively? What patterns do you see over time, either with individuals or with the group? "Try It *Yourselves*: Make a Collective Commitment to Facilitating and Participating More Effectively" offers an idea for how a group could work towards new and better patterns of interaction.

Door #4: Address Meeting Dilemmas

The final entry point involves taking your meeting agenda dilemmas head-on. Consider the dilemmas we discussed in chapters 5 and 6. Sometimes dilemmas will vary from one meeting to the next; other times dilemmas can seem to persist across meetings. In either case, go through the lists of dilemmas to help you diagnose what is happening.

Then take a look at our ideas for addressing the dilemma, or better yet, come up with ideas of your own (see "Try It *Yourselves*: Make a Collective Commitment to Addressing A Meeting Dilemma"). If you don't find your particular dilemma discussed in this book, work together to try and put your finger on the nature of the tension you are feeling. Naming the problem is a first step in figuring out how to address it.

Try It *Yourselves*
Make a Collective Commitment to Facilitating and Participating More Effectively

1. Assemble a group of people from throughout your organization who have all read this book and done the " Try It Yourself" activities at the end of chapters 5 and 6.

2. Choose one of the tasks that the group is particularly interested in addressing: keeping to (and deviating from) the agenda, supporting full engagement, managing conflict, or maintaining awareness of the role you play.

3. Show people the top tips for facilitators and participants for that task (see the Quick Reference Guide in the Resources section). At the top of an index card, have people write "When I play the role of facilitator . . . " Below that, have them write the top tip that they most want to work on and the top tip that they would most appreciate participants working on. For example, if the group has agreed to address supporting full engagement, the index card may look like this:

> When I play the role of facilitator:
> I want to work on: making room for many voices
> I want participants to work on: being fully present

4. On the other side of the index card, have people write "When I play the role of participant . . ." Below that, have them write the top tip that they most want to work on and the top tip that they would most appreciate facilitators working on. For example, if the group has agreed to address supporting full engagement, the index card may look like this:

> When I play the role of participant:
> I want to work on: building on the ideas of others
> I want facilitators to work on: using visual cues
> and tools

5. Have everyone share their requests of "I want facilitators to work on . . . " so that facilitators can use the list of requests to inform their planning.

6. Have people bring their cards to all meetings for two weeks. At the beginning of each meeting, have the facilitator say what he or she is working on as a facilitator and what she would like to see participants do. Then have participants share what is written on the "When I play the role of participant . . . "side of their cards. The first time the group gets together, this may take a few minutes, but after a while people will know what the others are working on, so this is likely to go quickly.

7. At the end of each meeting, include time for reflection about evidence that facilitators and participants were trying to play their roles more effectively.

8. At the end of two weeks, reconvene the group to discuss how it went. What happened? What should happen next?

Try It *Yourselves*
Make a Collective Commitment to Addressing a Meeting Dilemma

1. Assemble a group of people from throughout your organization who have all read this book and done the "Try It Yourself" activities at the end of chapters 5 and 6.

2. Give everyone three to five sticky notes. Have people silently and independently write one meeting dilemma that they think is important for your organization to address on each note. To keep everyone's mind open, start this activity by having people think broadly about issues that they care about without referring to the list of common dilemmas from this book.

3. If you have a large group, have people form subgroups of about five people. Give each group a piece of chart paper and ask them to work together to sort their dilemmas into categories, and give each category a name.

4. For each category, have the subgroup propose a way of addressing that type of dilemma. At this point, people can review the common dilemmas (see the Quick Reference Guide in the Resources section for a reproducible handout) to see if there are any ideas that would be helpful.

5. If you have a large group, have each subgroup report out one category of dilemma together with their ideas for addressing that type of dilemma.

6. Pick one of the dilemmas and commit to addressing it with specific action steps.

7. Reconvene in two to four weeks. What happened when you tried to address this dilemma? What should happen next?

WORDS TO THE WISE

We hope that you are now feeling better equipped to plan and have not just *one* effective meeting, but a series of them. Just like in classrooms, one fabulous session can be fun, stimulating, and rich—but it's not nearly as powerful as a sequence of sessions that build on one another toward an important goal. We opened this book by saying that the agenda for a good meeting is like a lesson plan for a good class. Extending this metaphor, the agendas from a series of related meetings are like the syllabus for a course. Learning happens over time as part of a coherent set of experiences that lead somewhere valuable.

Another way to think of your collaborative meetings is as stepping-stones across a river—places where you and your colleagues make meaningful progress toward your goal, and where you regroup between leaps, giving yourselves the time you need to catch your balance, assess your options, and chart your course. In order to get to a better place with learning and teaching, sometimes you need to cross some pretty challenging waters.

After reading chapter 1, you may have determined that, in general, you're not getting your money's worth with all your meetings. You've invested in the stepping-stones, and while some may provide reasonable support, others might be wobbly, unnecessary, or even downright dangerous.

In chapters 2 through 6, you may have made important headway in figuring out how to set a particular stepping-stone so that it provides a solid place from which your team can make progress. Improving the quality of the planning, facilitation, and participation in a single meeting is useful. However, if you think of each meeting in isolation, you might succeed in creating several very firm stepping-stones, but have no guarantee that they will take you where you want to go. Unless each stable stone has a clear connection to all the others, you and your colleagues could find yourself jumping around from one nice, solid rock to another without getting any closer toward the prize on the other shore.

We began this book describing our vision for a coherent symmetry throughout the entire educational enterprise in how people work together. This should apply right through to the student level, where there is a growing consensus in the importance of regular practice in solving complex problems and communicating ideas. To give students these opportunities, teachers, administrators, policy makers, and community members need personal experience with engaging in these types of activities as well. Making the tasks in meetings challenging can have a ripple effect that is felt in students' daily lives.

When we build strategies for effective collaboration into our work with educators, teachers quickly adapt those strategies for use in their own classrooms. For example, teachers we have worked with from Australia to West Texas are now building the Plus/Delta Protocol into their lesson plans because they have experienced how this strategy for seeking feedback can have a powerful impact on engagement and productivity in their meetings with adults.

Wise meetings also help people develop higher-functioning teams, one of the key components of an effective organization and an essential skill for living in our global, networked world. Research on teams says that what differentiates a group from a team is shared purpose and tasks toward that purpose. Any group that is meeting regularly has the opportunity to become more teamlike as it develops that shared purpose and works toward meeting it.

The tools and tips in this book are designed to help you focus your energy and attention on the crucial work of improving learning. Adapt, modify, and experiment with these resources to make meetings wiser in your organization. The goal is not a tightly scripted meeting where everything runs like clockwork. In many settings, alarms sounding every few minutes and obsessive note taking on every topic would be a recipe for squelched creativity and heightened anxiety. A good meeting, like a good classroom experience, has a clear purpose, a thoughtful strategy for achieving it, and a group working together to achieve that purpose.

None of us became educators because we wanted to become champion meeting planners, facilitators, or participants—but wise meetings will help deliver on a determination to improving learning and teaching for all the students in our care. And as you and your colleagues get better at building a pathway of solid stepping-stones, don't be surprised if you find that you end up designing creative ways to get to an even more ambitious destination than you originally hoped for.

As you experiment and improve, please share your insights at http://www.gse.harvard.edu/meetingwise. There is a whole world waiting to learn from what you discover, and a whole generation of children whose learning trajectories will soar if the adults who serve them treat their collaborative time as an investment in learning.

SECTION **III** **RESOURCES**

SELECTED READINGS

The following readings have helped shape our understanding about . . .

Coping with the demands of a complex world

Csikszentmihaly, M. *Flow: The Psychology of Optimal Experience.* New York: Harper & Row, 1990.

Gawande, A. *The Checklist Manifesto: How to Get Things Right.* New York: Metropolitan Books, 2009.

Murnane, R.J. and F. Levy. *Teaching the New Basic Skills: Principles for Educating Children to Thrive in a Changing Economy.* New York: Free Press, 1996.

Working collaboratively

DuFour, R., R. DuFour, R. Eaker, and T. Many. *Learning by Doing: A Handbook for Professional Learning Communities at Work.* Bloomington, IN: Solution Tree, 2006.

Garmston, R. and B. Wellman. *The Adaptive School: A Sourcebook for Developing Collaborative Groups.* Norwood, MA: Christopher-Gordon, 1999.

Kegan, R. and L. Lahey. *How the Way We Talk Can Change the Way We Work: Seven Languages for Transformation.* San Francisco: Jossey-Bass, 2001.

McDonald, J.P., N. Mohr, A. Dichter, and E.C. McDonald. *The Power of Protocols: An Educator's Guide to Better Practice*, 3rd edition. New York: Teachers College Press, 2013.

Building a learning organization

Garvin, D.A., A.C. Edmondson, and F. Gino. "Is Yours a Learning Organization?" *Harvard Business Review*, March 2008.

Senge, P., N. Cambron-McCabe, T. Lucas, B. Smith, J. Dutton, and A. Kleiner. *Schools That Learn: A Fifth Discipline Handbook for Educators, Parents, and Everyone Who Cares About Education* (updated and revised). New York: Crown Business, 2012.

SELECTED PROTOCOLS

AS DESCRIBED IN CHAPTER 3, discussion protocols are handy tools for structuring conversations so that all participants engage meaningfully in advancing meeting objectives and contribute to helping the group achieve its broader purpose.

In the following pages we offer detailed protocols for doing two things that are essential to having wise meetings: setting norms (which typically happens at the first in a series of meetings) and obtaining feedback (which can happen at the end of every meeting). We also provide some general strategies for getting a meeting started, making decisions, and energizing a group. For additional information about protocols, please note that:

The School Reform Initiative website offers a wide range of protocols on a variety of topics: http://www.schoolreforminitiative.org/.

The Data Wise Project website offers protocols for engaging educators in collaborative inquiry around improving teaching and learning: www.gse.harvard.edu/datawise.

The Teachers College Press website (http://www.tcpress.com/pdfs/mcdonaldprot.pdf) provides instructions for the protocols referenced in: J.P. McDonald, N. Mohr, A. Dichter, and E.C. McDonald, *The Power of Protocols: An Educator's Guide to Better Practice*. (New York: Teachers College Press, 2013).

✳ NORM-SETTING PROTOCOL

Purpose

This protocol helps a group agree to the ground rules for how they will behave during meetings.

Notes

* As described below, this protocol can take 25–30 minutes. It can also be shortened considerably if the group starts with a proposed list of norms and a clarification of what each means (see chapter 4 for a sample list). If you take this approach, you can skip steps 2 through 5 below.

* Give each participant an index card.

* Have chart paper or a projection screen available for capturing norms.

Steps

1. **1 MINUTE**. Explain that in order to work together effectively over time on challenging issues, a group needs to agree on how people will behave during meetings.

2. **2 MINUTES**. Give participants time to write silently and independently on their index cards the behaviors that they would like to see the group follow.

3. **2 MINUTES**. Give participants time to share their proposed norms with a partner. (This helps "prime the pump" for the group brainstorming that follows; by getting everyone talking right away, you make it more likely that the norm-setting conversation will not be dominated by a few voices.)

4. **5 MINUTES**. Have participants call out norms as you capture the brain-stormed list on chart paper or on a screen that everyone can see.

5. **5–10 MINUTES**. Allow participants to ask for clarification of what a norm on the list means, or to propose collapsing two or more norms into one. Explain that having a manageable number of norms (three to seven is ideal) makes it more likely that the group will be able to remember and internalize the list.

6. **1 MINUTE.** Have participants look at the revised list with a partner and discuss whether they are not able to live with any of the norms.

7. **1–5 MINUTES.** Have participants share with the group any norms they cannot live with and their rationale. Revise or eliminate norms until everyone is comfortable with the list.

8. **2 MINUTES.** Discuss what the group commits to doing if a norm is violated.

9. **1 MINUTE.** Explain where the list of norms will "live" and identify a time in the future when the group will revisit the list to assess (1) how well the norms are being followed and (2) whether the list needs to be revised.

Tips

* When allowing time for clarification of what norms mean, it can be helpful to ask "What would it look like and feel like if this norm were followed?"

* If the group has substantial experience with norm setting, it can be good to acknowledge that up front. Sometimes asking people to describe their past experience can help get out into the open some frustrations people may feel with the whole norm-setting process. If there is a sentiment that norms are a "touchy-feely" thing that groups do on the first day they work together and then never return to again, you may want to challenge participants to figure out what the group could do to avoid that outcome in the present situation.

* It can be helpful to have the norms "live" in multiple places, including on a poster in the meeting room, in a footer on the agenda template, or even on tents on each table. The most important place, of course, is in people's hearts and minds. As facilitator, when you see a norm being followed, it can be helpful for you to point that out explicitly so that the group becomes aware of the extent to which norms are alive in the group.

✳ PLUS/DELTA PROTOCOL

Purpose

This protocol helps a group develop a shared sense of responsibility for having effective meetings by engaging everyone in assessing what worked well in a meeting and what they would have liked to change. By capturing reflections within the meeting, it offers facilitators—and participants—immediate feedback on how to improve subsequent meetings.

Notes

* It is possible to do this protocol in five minutes (as shown below). However, it can be helpful to allow up to ten minutes for the protocol in longer meetings, where you may feel it is important for individuals to have more time for quiet reflection, or in large meetings, where you may want the group to be able to hear reflections from a greater number of participants.

* Give each participant an index card.

* Project on a screen or draw on chart paper the following chart:

+ WHAT WORKED WELL	Δ WHAT TO CHANGE NEXT TIME

Steps

1. **1 MINUTE.** Explain that a powerful way of improving collaborative work is to gather feedback about how the meeting went, and use this information to make future meetings more effective. Review the objectives of the meeting so that everyone is reminded of what the meeting was designed to achieve.

2. **2 MINUTES.** Show participants the chart and ask them to copy it onto their index card. Ask them to silently and independently write down what worked well in the meeting (under the plus column) and what they would have liked to change (under the delta column).

3.   **1 MINUTE**. Ask for a few volunteers to share pluses and capture the responses on a chart or screen.

4.   **1 MINUTE**. Then ask for deltas and write those responses on the chart. Collect all index cards at the end of the protocol.

Tips

If participants offer very general comments that do not provide much guidance about what is working or how to improve:

* Ask people to be specific and descriptive in their comments. Instead of stating that the meeting was "really helpful," explain that you would like them to describe *what about it* was really helpful. You may want to encourage participants to start each plus with a word ending in "ing." Pluses such as "getting the agenda well in advance of the meeting," "having an opportunity to work in small groups with people I don't usually talk with," and "adjusting our objectives to take into account new information" will give a much richer picture about what people value in meetings.

* Similarly, you may want to ask people to phrase their deltas as verbs in the command form. This helps ensure that the deltas are not a list of gripes but rather a list of specific suggestions for what to do differently. "Allow more time to review next steps," "Use a more transparent process for making decisions," and "Provide more opportunities for movement" are deltas that will give you a clear sense of what needs to be changed.

If participants are hesitant to provide deltas:

* Remind them that deltas will help the group have better meetings (and perhaps put a delta of your own on the list to get things started).

* Build in time to allow people to share their deltas with a partner; sometimes this helps generate some energy and confidence around articulating areas for improvement.

* If you begin each meeting by reviewing the previous meeting's pluses and deltas and explaining how the meeting will take them into account, you are likely to find participants are more forthcoming with their comments at future meetings.

If you are running short on time:

* Ask individuals to write their pluses and deltas on index cards and leave them in the middle of table or hand them in as they leave the meeting. This method allows the comments to be more anonymous, which in some situations may lead to more candid feedback.

* Skip the index cards and instead have everyone offer pluses and deltas out loud. This method works for small groups and when you don't feel it is essential to get feedback from each individual.

* If you are using a shared electronic agenda during the meeting, ask people to type pluses and deltas directly into the document.

* Invite people to send feedback electronically after the meeting.

If you have a lot of participants:

* Use polling software to create a survey that contains two open-ended questions: "What worked well in this meeting?" and "What would you have liked to change about this meeting?" Have participants complete the survey in the last few minutes of the meeting, perhaps leaving a little time for people to share out a few of their entries. The advantage of collecting data in this way is that all of the responses are captured electronically, making it easy to analyze and share.

PROTOCOLS IN BRIEF

PROTOCOL FOR GETTING STARTED

One simple protocol that we use at the beginning of every meeting is simply called the "The Check-In." We discovered years ago that our meeting participants (including us!) always wanted to connect with one another on a human level before diving into the work at hand. So we introduced the check-in as a regular, time-bound way to honor that impulse (and to make sure that we budgeted for the three to ten minutes that it requires).

When we have fewer than 10 meeting participants, we typically start by going around the room and having each person offer a 30- to 60-second comment about how he or she doing, either personally or with respect to the content at hand. Sometimes we phrase it as asking each person to offer a "highlight of the week." Getting everyone's voice in the room early in the session can help reduce anxiety about participating as the meeting unfolds and can help people see their connections to one another and to the work. When the group is larger, we will often invite people to do a quick check-in with the person seated next to them, or even find someone across the room that they haven't yet met but would like to.

PROTOCOLS FOR MAKING DECISIONS

Frequently meetings call for making decisions—sometimes big, sometimes small. One way of quickly gauging where people are on an issue is known as "Fist to Five." The facilitator makes a statement, such as "I think we have enough information to move to the next phase of the work" and participants show their agreement with the statement by holding up no fingers (a "fist") if they completely disagree all the way up to five fingers if they completely agree, This allows participants to see where their colleagues stand. We typically ask to hear from the people who hold up fewer than three fingers so that we get a sense of what the concerns are.

A more time-intensive approach involves going around the room and asking participants to weigh in with one or two sentences that describe where they stand on an issue and their rationale.

When the decision to be made involves choosing among multiple competing priorities, it can be helpful to list each option on chart paper and give participants one to three stickers that they can use to register their vote(s). This approach has the advantage of providing some anonymity, which can be helpful in circumstances where power dynamics might interfere with candid responses. An electronic version of this approach can involve using handheld devices to allow for real-time voting on options.

PROTOCOLS FOR ENERGIZING A ROOM

During long meetings, it can be well worth the time to stop for a quick pick-me-up. And the surest way of getting the energy flowing is to get people moving! In large groups where people do not yet know one another well, a simple strategy is to offer two minutes for people to do a "friendly handshake." The task is simple: all people need to do is stand up and try to shake as many hands in as they can in two minutes. This works particularly well when people are wearing nametags, so that with each handshake, participants can say "Good morning, Dory" or "Good afternoon, Liza" as they go.

If you want people to stay close to their seats for your energizer, try having people sing "Row, Row, Row Your Boat" as a group, dropping the last word each time through (e.g., don't say "dream" the first time; don't say "a dream" the second time; don't say "but a dream" the third time). It helps to have the words written on chart paper or some visual, and then to cover the words with your hand the first few times through until people get the hang of it. Stop when you run out of words.

Row, row, row your boat
Gently down the stream
Merrily, merrily, merrily, merrily
Life is but a dream.

Another song that can bring some life into a sagging meeting is "My Bonnie." Start by asking for a volunteer to sing the song to make sure everyone knows the tune. You may also want to project the words on a screen:

My Bonnie lies over the ocean
My Bonnie lies over the sea
My Bonnie lies over the ocean
Oh bring back my Bonnie to me
Bring back, bring back,
Oh bring back my Bonnie to me, to me
Bring back, bring back,
Oh bring back my Bonnie to me.

Then instruct the group to sing along, changing position any time they sing a word that contains the letter "B." So the first time they sing the word "Bonnie," they stand up, the next time they sit back down again. By the time they get to the fourth and fifth lines, they'll be bouncing up and down (and smiling and laughing, if experience is any guide). You may be amazed to see how a little oxygen wakes people up and gets them ready to take on the next part of the meeting.

If you've got enough time and you would like to really get the room going, try a Rock, Paper, Scissors tournament. Start by reviewing the rules: People put their right hand behind their back as they look at their partner and say the words "Rock, Paper, Scissors, Shoot!" On the word "Shoot," each person brings his or her hand to the front formed either as rock (a fist), a piece of paper (a flat hand), or scissors (second and third fingers making a "V"). If both participants show the same symbol, they repeat until they have two different symbols. The winner is determined as follows:

Rock crushes scissors.

Paper covers rock.

Scissors cuts paper.

The loser then becomes the winner's fan, and helps the winner find the winner from another pair to take on. Once a winner from that competition is determined, everyone else in the foursome goes on to cheer the new winner. This goes on until there are only two people left to compete, each with his or her own cheering section. By this time, some positive energy will have been generated, and when the tournament is over, everyone will be ready to reengage in the meeting with newfound vigor.

QUICK REFERENCE GUIDE*

---

* For electronic versions of these documents, please go to http://www.gse.harvard.edu /meetingwise.

The Meeting Wise Checklist—Full Version

		YES	NO
PURPOSE	**1.** Have we identified clear and important meeting *objectives* that contribute to the goal of improving learning?	☐	☐
	2. Have we established the *connection* between the work of this and other meetings in the series?	☐	☐
PROCESS	**3.** Have we incorporated *feedback* from previous meetings?	☐	☐
	4. Have we chosen challenging *activities* that advance the meeting objectives and engage all participants?	☐	☐
	5. Have we assigned *roles*, including facilitator, timekeeper, and note taker?	☐	☐
	6. Have we built in time to identify and commit to *next steps*?	☐	☐
	7. Have we built in time for *assessment* of what worked and what didn't in the meeting?	☐	☐
PREPARATION	**8.** Have we gathered or developed *materials* (drafts, charts, etc.) that will help to focus and advance the meeting objectives?	☐	☐
	9. Have we determined what, if any, *pre-work* we will ask participants to do before the meeting?	☐	☐
PACING	**10.** Have we put *time allocations* to each activity on the agenda?	☐	☐
	11. Have we ensured that we will address the *primary objective* early in the meeting?	☐	☐
	12. Is it *realistic* that we could get through our agenda in the time allocated?	☐	☐

Meeting Wise Agenda Checklist—Short Version

		YES	NO
PURPOSE	**1.** Objectives	☐	☐
	2. Connection	☐	☐
PROCESS	**3.** Feedback	☐	☐
	4. Activities	☐	☐
	5. Roles	☐	☐
	6. Next steps	☐	☐
	7. Assessment	☐	☐
PREPARATION	**8.** Materials	☐	☐
	9. Pre-work	☐	☐
PACING	**10.** Time allocations	☐	☐
	11. Primary objective	☐	☐
	12. Is it realistic?	☐	☐

Meeting Wise Agenda Template

MEETING AGENDA
[date], [start time] – [end time]
[location]

TOPIC:	Attendees: Facilitator: Note taker: Timekeeper:

MEETING OBJECTIVES:
- [objective 1]
- [objective 2]
- [objective 3]

TO PREPARE FOR THIS MEETING, PLEASE:
- Read this agenda [optional: and reply to (name) with feedback by (date)]
- [other pre-work task]

Schedule [XX minutes]

TIME	MINUTES	ACTIVITY
X:XX-X:XX	X	Check-in and review objectives of this meeting and how they connect to the objectives for our remaining team meetings this year
X:XX-X:XX	X	Review next steps from our previous meeting
X:XX-X:XX	X	Review plus/deltas from our previous meeting | Plus	Delta | |---|---|
• [pluses from previous meeting]	• [deltas from previous meeting]	
X:XX-X:XX	X	[objective 1]
X:XX-X:XX	X	[objective 2]
X:XX-X:XX	X	[objective 3]
X:XX-X:XX	X	Review next steps
X:XX-X:XX	X	Assess what worked well about this meeting and what we would have liked to change | Plus	Delta | |---|---|
•	•	

Foundational and Recurring Meeting Setup Tasks

FOUNDATIONAL SETUP TASKS	RECURRING SETUP TASKS

• Set group norms
• Acknowledge work style preferences
• Develop agenda template
• Make documentation plan
	• Send agenda to participants
	• Arrange logistics
	  • Space
	  • Supplies
	  • Name cards
	  • Refreshments
	  • Technology
	• Get your head ready

Top Tips for Having a Wise Meeting

ACTION	FOR FACILITATORS	FOR PARTICIPANTS
1 Keeping to (and Deviating from) the Agenda	• Start on time • Let purpose rule • Clarify next steps and decision processes • Listen to feedback • End on time	• Understand purpose • Leave your agenda at home • Use assigned roles
2 Supporting Full Engagement	• Welcome participants • Clarify roles • Check on preparation • Make room for many voices • Use visual tools	• Do unto others • Be fully present • Use people's names • Build on ideas
3 Managing Conflict	• Set the tone • Review norms	• Be courageous • Challenge ideas, not people
4 Maintaining Awareness of the Role You Play	• Choose your seat deliberately • Model being a learner	• Be mindful of preferences • Provide feedback

Common Dilemmas		
TASK	**FOR FACILITATORS**	**FOR PARTICIPANTS**
1 Keeping to (and Deviating from) the Agenda	• You're not ready at start time • The conversation wanders • A new topic comes up • An agenda item is taking too long • You can't finish on time	• You think the meeting is serving the wrong purpose • There's an elephant in the room
2 Supporting Full Engagement	• There's silence • The activity isn't working • You're too much at the center of things • There's an energy lull • Some or all people are participating virtually	• You're unprepared • You're talking too much • You're talking too little • You're participating virtually
3 Managing Conflict	• People don't know how to disagree • Norms are violated • One person is the problem • The culture is the problem • You're uncomfortable	• Everyone is playing nice • Someone else is upset • You're upset • You want to help the facilitator • You want to challenge the facilitator
4 Maintaining Awareness of the Role You Play	• You have less authority than others • You have more authority than others	• You have significant positional authority • You're more comfortable facilitating than participating

NOTES

Introduction

1. K. P. Boudett, E. City, and R. J. Murnane, eds., *Data Wise: A Step-by-Step Guide to Using Assessment Results to Improve Teaching and Learning* (Cambridge, MA: Harvard Education Press, 2005; revised and expanded edition published in 2013).

2. Instructional rounds is a practice based on medical rounds; it includes collaborative observation and protocols for debriefing, with an aim of building collective understanding and language around learning and teaching as part of an overall improvement strategy. For more information, see E. City, R. F. Elmore, S. E. Fiarman, and L. Teitel, *Instructional Rounds in Education: A Network Approach to Improving Teaching and Learning* (Cambridge, MA: Harvard Education Press, 2009).

Chapter 1

1. P. Senge, et al., *Schools That Learn: A Fifth Discipline Handbook for Educators, Parents, and Everyone Who Cares About Education* (New York: Crown Business, 2000).

2. D. Garvin, A.C. Edmondson, and F. Gino, "Is Yours a Learning Organization?" *Harvard Business Review*, March 2008.

3. M. Csikszentmihaly, *Flow: The Psychology of Optimal Experience* (New York: Harper & Row, 1990).

Chapter 2

1. A. Gawande, *The Checklist Manifesto: How to Get Things Right* (New York: Metropolitan Books, 2009), 36.

2. L. Anderson, et al. *A Taxonomy for Learning, Teaching, and Assessing: A Revision of Bloom's Taxonomy of Educational Objectives* (New York: Longman, 2001).

3. *Technical tip:* To embed a link to a document within an agenda, select the text from the agenda that you want to link to the other document (for example, in "Please read the draft proposal," select "draft proposal" or "proposal"). Then click the "Insert" tab, click the "Hyperlink" option, and paste in the URL of the document. It's that easy!

Chapter 3

1. For instructions about how to facilitate this protocol, please see the School Reform Initiative website: http://schoolreforminitiative.org/doc /lasw_equity.pdf.
2. For instructions about how to facilitate this protocol, please see the School Reform Initiative website: http://schoolreforminitiative.org/doc /consultancy.pdf.
3. For more information about this protocol, please see M. Correa-Connolly, *99 Activities and Greetings* (Turners Falls, MA: Northeast Foundation for Children, 2004), 59.

Chapter 4

1. For instructions about how to facilitate this protocol, see the School Reform Initiative website: http://schoolreforminitiative.org/doc/compass _points.pdf.
2. For more information about using this particular strategy for understanding individual work style preferences, see http://truecolorsintl.com.
3. See, for example, Boudett, K. P., City, E. A., & Russell, M. K. (2010). *Key Elements of Observing Practice: A Data Wise DVD and Facilitator's Guide.* Cambridge, MA: Harvard Education Press which includes examples of ten different agendas and accompanying facilitator notes.

Chapter 5

1. Our colleague Dick Murnane often says this at meetings where people are just beginning to work with one another. It helps participants konw that rigorous thought is encouraged.

Chapter 6

1. http://www.youtube.com/watch?v=QhXJe8ANws8&feature=em-share _video_user.
2. Robert Garmston and Bruce Wellman, *The Adaptive School: A Sourcebook for Developing Collaborative Groups* (Norwood, MA: Christopher-Gordon,1999), 37.
3. R. DuFour et al., *Learning by Doing: A Handbook for Professional Learning Communities at Work* (Bloomington, IN: Solution Tree, 2006), 106.
4. Ibid.

ABOUT THE AUTHORS

Kathryn Parker Boudett is Lecturer on Education and the Director of the Data Wise Project at the Harvard Graduate School of Education, where she supports educators in cultivating a systematic approach to improving classroom practice through sustained collaborative inquiry. Kathy teaches on-campus and online courses focused on the skills and habits of mind essential to improving learning and teaching (and does her best to ensure that every class she teaches and meeting she runs is as wise as it can be!). She is co-editor of *Data Wise: A Step-By-Step Guide to Using Assessment Results to Improve Teaching and Learning—Revised and Expanded Edition* with Richard Murnane and Elizabeth City (Harvard Education Press, 2013); *Data Wise in Action: Stories of Schools Using Data to Improve Teaching and Learning* (Harvard Education Press, 2007) with Jennifer Steele; and co-author of *Key Elements of Observing Practice: A Data Wise Facilitator's Guide and DVD* (Harvard Education Press, 2010) with Elizabeth City and Marcia Russell. Kathy holds a PhD in Public Policy from the Harvard Graduate School of Arts and Sciences and a BA in Economics from Yale University.

✳ ✳ ✳

Elizabeth A. City is Lecturer on Education and Director of the Doctor of Education Leadership (EdLD) Program at the Harvard Graduate School of Education, where she helps educators develop the skills, knowledge, mindsets, imagination, and efficacy to improve the way they and their colleagues serve every child's learning needs. Liz has served as a teacher, instructional coach, principal, and consultant, in each role focused on helping all children, and the educators who work with them, realize their full potential.

Her publications include: *Data Wise: A Step-by-Step Guide to Using Assessment Results to Improve Teaching and Learning—Revised and Expanded Edition*, coedited with Kathryn Parker Boudett and Richard J. Murnane (Harvard Education Press, 2013); *Strategy in Action: How School Systems Can Support Powerful Learning and Teaching*, coauthored with Rachel E. Curtis (Harvard Education Press, 2009); *Instructional Rounds in Education: A Network Approach to Improving Teaching and Learning*, coauthored with Richard F. Elmore, Sarah E. Fiarman, and Lee Teitel (Harvard Education Press, 2009); *Resourceful Leadership: Tradeoffs and Tough Decisions on the Road to School Improvement* (Harvard Education Press, 2008); and *The Teacher's Guide to Leading Student-Centered Discussions: Talking about Texts in the Classroom*, coauthored with Michael S. Hale (Corwin Press, 2006). She holds a doctorate in Administration, Planning, and Social Policy from the Harvard Graduate School of Education.

INDEX